SYNESIUS OF CYRENE:

HIS LIFE AND WRITINGS.

BIRMINGHAM:
PRINTED BY HALL AND ENGLISH, HIGH STREET.

SYNESIUS OF CYRENE

HIS LIFE AND WRITINGS.

BY

J. C. NICOL, B.A.,

FELLOW OF TRINITY HALL, CAMBRIDGE.

AN ESSAY WHICH OBTAINED THE HULSEAN PRIZE
FOR THE YEAR 1886.

" ἅπας γὰρ βίος ἀρετῆς ὕλη."

Cambridge:
E. JOHNSON, 30, TRINITY STREET.
1887.

TO MY FATHER

A SMALL TRIBUTE OF GRATITUDE

AND AFFECTION.

CLAUSES *directed by the* FOUNDER *to be always prefixed to the* HULSEAN DISSERTATION.

CLAUSES from the WILL of the Rev. JOHN HULSE, late of Elworth, in the County of Chester, clerk, deceased: dated the twenty-first day of July, in the year of our Lord one thousand seven hundred and seventy-seven; expressed in the words of the Testator, as he, in order to prevent mistakes, thought proper to draw and write the same himself, and directed that such clauses should every year be printed, to the intent that the several persons whom it might concern and be of service to, might know that there were such special donations or endowments left for the encouragement of Piety and Learning, in an age so unfortunately addicted to Infidelity and Luxury, and that others might be invited to the like charitable, and, as he humbly hoped, seasonable and useful Benefactions.

He directs that certain rents and profits (now amounting to about a hundred pounds yearly) be paid to such learned and ingenious person, in the University of Cambridge, under the degree of Master of Arts, as shall compose, for that year, the best Dissertation, in the English language, on the Evidences in general, or on the Prophecies or Miracles in particular, or any other particular Argument whether the same be direct or collateral proofs of the Christian Religion, in order to evince its truth and excellence; the subject of which Dissertation shall be given out by the Vice-Chancellor, and the Masters of Trinity and Saint John's, his Trustees, or by some of them, on New Year's Day annually; and that such Dissertation as shall be by them, or any two of them, on Christmas Day annually, the best approved, be also printed, and the expense defrayed out of the Author's income under his Will, and the remainder given to him on Saint John the Evangelist's Day following; and he who shall be so rewarded, shall not be admitted at any future time as a Candidate again in the same way, to the intent that others may be invited and encouraged to write on so sacred and sublime a subject.

He also desires, that immediately following the last of the clauses relating to the prize Dissertation, this invocation may be added: "May the Divine Blessing for ever go along with all my benefactions; and may the Greatest and the Best of Beings, by His all-wise Providence and gracious influence, make the same effectual to His own glory, and the good of my fellow-creatures!"

PREFACE.

IN the biography of Synesius I have mainly adopted the arrangement and chronology of Druon (Études sur la Vie et les Œuvres de Synésius), verifying his references throughout, and occasionally differing from his conclusions. Tillemont's admirable life of Synesius, which was only accessible to me when my work was nearly over, is the source of several corrections and additions, especially in the historical portion of the essay. Three articles by Kraus in the Tübingen Theologische Quartalschrift (1865-1866) and a short review by Hefele of the work of Krabinger were especially useful in the discussion of Synesius' standpoint as a philosopher and as a Christian. Druon, Tillemont, and Kraus, therefore, are the writers to whom I owe most, but whatever I derived from other sources I have acknowledged I think in every case. I should add that Miss Gardiner's interesting book on the subject has enabled me since writing the essay to correct one or two omissions in the narrative of Synesius' life.

With regard to the question of originality, I can only say that I have read the works of Synesius* for myself and tried to form an independent judgment.

Lastly, my best thanks are due to Mr. A. W. W. Dale, of Trinity Hall, for his kind assistance and advice in my final revision and in the correction of the proofs.

* The references throughout are to the edition of Synesius' Works in Vol. lxv, of Migne's Patrology.

CONTENTS.

ἅπας γὰρ βίος ἀρετῆς ὕλη.

De Providentia.

SYNESIUS OF CYRENE.

375—397.

INTRODUCTION.

IT was some fifty years before the birth of Synesius, when the Emperor Constantine made his great attempt to reorganize the Roman Empire, and, by infusing a feeling of unity into the heterogeneous nations of which it was composed, to fend off for a time the perils which threatened from without. His political measures, especially as regarded the government of the provinces, were well meant and ought to have alleviated the hardships of the provincials: but the whole system was corrupt; and reforms, however excellent in theory, are useless unless supported by a healthy public opinion. Far more important, because it was more far-reaching in its results, was the adoption of Christianity as the State religion: and though the immediate consequences of this step did not tend to the unity of thought and action which was Constantine's aim, still this was the ultimate influence of Christianity, partly as raising the old civilization from its moral degradation, and still more as humanizing the new races who were soon to give fresh life and vigour to a decaying world.

The advantage to Christianity from a spiritual point of view was however a doubtful one—as Gibbon puts it, "the piercing eye of ambition and avarice soon discovered that the profession of Christianity might contribute to the interest of the present as well as of a future life."[*] The hope of wealth and the example of an Emperor were

[*] Gibbon, c. xx., p. 165.

powerful incentives to conversion : and the Church must
have been flooded with devotees of more than doubtful
sincerity.

There was yet another insidious element of evil in the new
order of things. As Paganism declined, the Church grew
in wealth and influence. A Spiritual Power grew up beside
the Temporal : the high offices of the Church were sought
after by unscrupulous men for purposes of ambition, and
"the interested views, the selfish and angry passions, the
"arts of perfidy and dissimulation, the open and even bloody
"violence which had formerly disgraced the freedom of
"election in the Commonwealths of Greece and Rome, too
"often influenced the choice of the successors of the
"Apostles."*

Another feature of the age was the violence of its
controversies, especially of that famous controversy which
raged over the Arian heresy, and lasted through the greater
part of the fourth century ; being really at bottom an
epitome of the struggle between Christianity and Paganism
disguised in Christian forms ; between a true Monotheistic
religion and an exaggerated Monotheism which led back
necessarily to the Polytheism of the old mythologies.

For Paganism died very hard, and the orthodoxy of
Constantine was followed by a natural reaction in the
attempt of Julian to resuscitate the old creeds. But his
influence was wholly transitory and exerted in a falling
cause. The decrees of Theodosius (378-395) gave a fresh
blow to the weakened forces of Paganism, and though the
worship of the gods lingered in the country districts well on
into the fifth century, still at the time of Synesius' birth
Christianity was the prevailing religion of the ancient
world, and Greek thought, which had been declining since
the days of Plotinus, offered but slight resistance to its

* Gibbon, c. xx., p. 171.

mightier rival. Such was the moral condition of the Empire. But serious though the dangers were that threatened from within, there was yet greater peril looming on the frontiers. A vast migration of the Huns, a pastoral race of central Asia, drove the Gothic tribes on the frontiers first to demand and then to enforce the support and patronage of Rome.

The inevitable collision soon came, and the defeat of Valens at Hadrianople threatened the immediate ruin of the Empire. The skilful Theodosius, however, by his courage and address, averted the catastrophe for a time ; but the admission of the Goths not only to the army but to the offices of State, was a policy fraught with danger for the future. The age was thus a period of marked transition in every way. The passing away of the old civilization was in process, but the new era was only beginning to dawn.

While Paganism was being eradicated, and before Christianity was fully installed in its place, morality must have suffered. The old foundations were tottering ; men felt the ground cut from under them. It was an age of weak faith, when the strong and hard made way, and the feeble went to the wall. The deterioration, too, of the Christian Ideal, though a necessary consequence of the Church's enhanced worldly power, was unfortunate at a time when a lofty ideal was sorely needed. The corruption and vice of the great cities were not appreciably lessened, and the oriental luxury of the Court did not help to remedy the evil. The death of Theodosius in 395 A.D., and the division of the Empire between his two indolent and incapable sons, seemed to pave the way for barbarian ascendency : nor need we wonder if, with such a court and such rulers, the outlying provinces were ground down, and neglected in their hour of need.

Into this age of decline and disorder—this period of transition from the old faith to the new—at a time when the old civilization with all its corruption and refinement seemed on the point of being merged in the onward-rushing tide of barbarism—Synesius was born.

SYNESIUS OF CYRENE.

Birth and
Birthplace
of S.

Synesius was born about the year* 375 A.D., in the city of Cyrene. His mother Cyrene, as he calls her,† had fallen on evil days in this later age. There had been a time when the city of Battus held her head high among the settlements of Greater Hellas. Pindar had sung the victories of her sovereigns: Aristippus and Carneades in philosophy, Callimachus in poetry, Eratosthenes in science, had made her name famous.

But the prosperity of the place declined, and towards the close of the fourth century, Ammianus Marcellinus‡ refers to Cyrene briefly as "urbs antiqua sed deserta."

Such was the birthplace of Synesius. His family was a noble one and linked him with the greater past. At a time when even the proudest of Rome's patricians could only date the rise of their family from the second century B.C.,‖ it was something to be able to claim as one's ancestor Eurysthenes who led the Dorians into Sparta :§ something, to see the honoured tombs of one's forefathers in the city they had founded.¶ Synesius had

---

* The date of Synesius' birth may be said to lie approximately between 370 and 375. Druon, p. 6., argues for the former ; Clausen for the latter date. He was made Bishop in the year 409-10—and the canonical age was thirty years—so that Clausen's date is early enough.

† Ep. 93., 232 A.

‡ A.M., xxii., 16, 4.

‖ Gibbon. Vol. III. c. xxxi.

§ Ep. 57.

¶ Ep. 124. τῶν παππων τοὺς τάφους οὐκ ἀτίμους ὀρῶν.

reason to be proud of his descent and he refers more than once to it.* Before entering, however, upon details as to his family, there are two points upon which stress must be laid,—the nature of his birthplace: the consequences of his descent. In an age of extraordinary corruption and unmentionable vice, it was no small matter to be brought up in the purity and seclusion of a country life, far from the degrading influences of the great cities. To this cause we may trace the manly simplicity, and the healthy love of sport which are so marked in Synesius' character.

And secondly, the accumulated influences and tendencies of so many generations were not to be lightly set aside. To this cause we must attribute the fact that Synesius was Greek to the core, Greek to the last.

He seems to have lost his parents while he was still young, for there is scarcely† any mention of them in his writings. His father was apparently a senator of Cyrene and a man of means—what would, in fact, be considered wealth in so poor a country. He must have been possessed of some culture, for the son speaks of the library his father had left him, and the additions he had made to it himself.‡ We may infer too from Ep. 123 that Synesius succeeded to an independence. "I am not rich," these are his words, "but what I have is ample for Pylaemenes "and for me."

There was an elder brother, Evoptius, to whom so many

His parents and family.

---

* In *Catastasis*, p. 301 D., with a vanity ludicrous at so serious a crisis.

† In Ep. 20 he mentions with respect one Theodosius who had won the regard of his *parents*.

‡ *Dion.* 59, C. I possess much less land than I received by inheritance, and the greater number of my slaves enjoy at the present time the same rights of citizenship as myself. I have neither money in coin, nor in jewels, left: what there was, I have laid out like Pericles, εἰς τὸ δέον: But I have many more books than my father left me.

of the letters are addressed ; and conjecture identifies him with the Evoptius who was Bishop of Ptolemais in 431 A.D. He lived at Alexandria and in Cyrene at different periods of his life, and was appointed senator in the latter town, a position of much care and responsibility, if we may judge from his brother's letter,* upbraiding Hesychius for the appointment. There was also a sister, Stratonice, who was married to Theodosius, an officer in the Imperial bodyguard. He refers to her in one of his letters† and quotes the inscription written by himself upon her statue.

τῆς χρυσῆς εἰκὼν ἡ Κύπριδος ἡ Στρατονίκης.

It would be easy to multiply the names of his friends and connections whose names occur from time to time in his letters, or who have letters actually addressed to them. As the more important, however, will necessarily come to light in the course of the narrative, further mention of them may be omitted here.

His early life and training. Of Synesius' early life and training we know little. He writes‡ to one Auxentius, reminding him of the nurture and education they had shared in common ; but his boyhood was probably, with this exception, a solitary time, and we may infer from a biographical allusion in the speech against Andronicus,‖ that he took little part in the ordinary pursuits and diversions of boys or young men. Apart however from any direct allusion, we should gather from his writings enough to prove that he was an ardent student of philosophy from the first His studies were doubtless relieved by the pleasures of the chase, and he certainly spent some portion of his youth in military

* Ep. 92. His brother seems to have fled the country rather than submit to τὴν ἄτοπον ζημίαν.

† Ep. 75.

‡ Ep. 60.

‖ Epp. 57, 193.

service,* and learned in the field lessons of skill and endurance that stood him in good stead in after life.

So the years passed by, till it was time to see the world and gain new experiences of life and thought—and he was naturally drawn to Alexandria, the centre of arts and learning in that age.

We cannot fix the precise date of Synesius' visit to His first visit to Alexandria, but he must have been quite young, probably Alexandria. not more than seventeen or eighteen years of age. To a lad who had been leading a quiet life in the midst of a remote country district the busy life of Alexandria must have been a strange experience. He would see the great Library; the Museum with its scientific treasures; he would be dazzled by the learned society into which he was plunged, and the strange phases of thought and mysticism which made Alexandria, from an intellectual point of view, the most cosmopolitan city of the ancient world. Sophists or teachers of every form of rhetoric and *belles-lettres* abounded, while above all the minor sects and *coteries*, were the leaders of thought who still upheld the system of the great Plotinus.

In strange contrast to all this pompous array of Hellenistic arts and learning, there was the Christian Church : no persecuted body in those days, but an active and bitter rival of the older Paganism, and now with a Theophilus at its head, inclined rather to reverse the old order of things and turn persecutor.

Somewhere about the time in fact of Synesius' visit 389 A.D. (probably a year or two earlier) a fanatical band of Christians had destroyed the Serapeum,† and disturbed the peace of the city by acts of riot and pillage.

---

* Ep. 127.
† Gibbon, Vol. III., c. xxviii.

But Synesius had no thought at this time for theological differences; he entered at once into the studies of the place, and devoted himself to literary *jeux d'esprit*, to the cultivation of eloquence on which he lays such stress in *The Dion*, and more especially to the pursuit of mathematics and philosophy.

Hypatia. Of all the teachers of Neo-Platonism, none was more famous at this time than Hypatia, the daughter of Theon, a mathematician of note. Clad in the robes of a philosopher, she took her seat in the professional chair, or even discussed theses as she walked through the streets surrounded like Socrates by a band of disciples and admirers. She was at once the centre and the oracle of the philosophical life of Alexandria.

A beautiful woman, learned and eloquent, could not fail to impress a youth, and a Greek youth like Synesius. He became one of Hypatia's most brilliant and favourite pupils; and the friendship between them, which was only severed by death, shows to us Synesius' character in the best light. Whether he survived his teacher and friend is a point that will need discussion later on. The fate* of Hypatia may be briefly stated here. Her influence was her ruin, for the jealousy between Orestes and Cyril, the Prefect of Egypt, and the Head of the Church, which rumour hinted might have been smoothed over by Hypatia's mediation, led to an outbreak of popular frenzy. She was dragged from her lecture room by a fanatic, one Peter the reader, and torn to pieces by the mob before the high altar of their Cathedral.

Such was the end of Hypatia. Meanwhile her influence† over Synesius was deep and lasting. He dedicates‡ his

* Socrates, Eccl. Hist., Bk. VII., 15.
† Ep. 136.
‡ Ep. 153.

works to her, and submits them to her criticism. In his letters he addresses her as μητὲρ καὶ ἀδελφὴ καὶ διδάσκαλε ; and when he is cast down to the depths of despair by the loss of his children and the impending ruin of his country, it is to her that he confides the burden of his woes and can only say with Homer—

εἰ δὲ θανόντων περ καταλήθοντ᾽ εἰν Ἀΐδαο,

even there I will remember my beloved Hypatia.*

Of the actual work done by Synesius at Alexandria there is no certain record ; but he must have paid special attention to the rhetorical art, for his fame on that score was well established and led to his being chosen by his countrymen to plead their cause before the Emperor. He must have paid some attention too to Mathematics, for he writes to Hesychius† reminding him that the sacred science of geometry had been their bond of union ; and we know that his fondness for mathematics led to his intimacy with Paeonius, to whom he presented an astronomical instrument of his own invention, accompanying the gift with a letter which expressed his opinion that Geometry and Arithmetic teach us the only sure and infallible rules for the discovery of truth.

There is a passage also at the close of *The Dion*‡ which refers probably to this period. Imitations of the style of the earlier writers were in especial vogue at Alexandria, and the tragedies and comedies which Synesius refers to so lightly were probably mere *tours de force*, the productions of an age when originality in literature was unfashionable and impossible. " Often have I vied with Tragedies in solemnity "and with Comedies in absurdity, adapting myself to the

---

* Ep. 124. Cf. Epp. 10 and 16.
† Ep. 92.
‡ *Dion*, p. 62.

"tone of the writer. You would have said I was a con-
"temporary, now of Cratinus and Crates, now of Diphilus
"and Philemon ; nor is there any form of metre or poetry
"to which I did not apply myself with success." There is
no other mention of these writings, and we may fairly conclude, apart from the tacit verdict of antiquity, that they
were not worth preserving.

He sails to Athens. Soon after this visit to Alexandria Synesius sailed to
Athens, not so much from a desire to complete his philosophical training as from the wish to place himself on a level
with those who had been there and assumed airs in consequence towards less-favoured and less-travelled students.
He speaks in amusing terms of their pretensions,* and
insinuates that they based their superiority not on any
clearer understanding of Aristotle and Plato, but solely
upon their having seen the groves of Academe and the
famous porch where Zeno sat. Whatever his object may
have been, he was disappointed. He says,† "The Athens of
"to-day has nothing in it to reverence, only the famous
"names and memories of what has been." It reminds him
of the skin of the victim when the sacrifice has been con-
sumed. Even the ποικίλη στοά of Zeno is a thing of the
past, for its pictures have gone. As for the philosophy of
the place, he dismisses it with a contemptuous allusion to
certain lecturers who filled their theatres by bribing pupils
His return to Cyrene. with pots of Hymettian honey. He returned from Athens
to Cyrene, and there gave himself up to a life of retirement
until the needs of his country forced upon him the duties
of patriotism.

* Ep. 54.
† Ep. 135.

CONSTANTINOPLE.

397—400.

THE EMBASSY TO ARCADIUS.

THE district of Cyrene, the Libyan Pentapolis, lying on the outskirts of the Empire, in an isolated position between Carthage and Alexandria, had been suffering for years from divers causes. The locusts had destroyed the crops ; earthquakes had wrought havoc in their towns ; and the misgovernment and rapacity of the provincial rulers had brought the country to the verge of ruin. Worst plague of all, the barbarians, robber tribes who seem to have been the Bedouin* of their age, harassed the country districts and left famine in their wake.

Under these circumstances, it was not surprising that the Senate of Cyrene† resolved to avail themselves of their privilege‡ and to send a remonstrance to the Emperor, with an appeal for troops and a remission of taxes. Synesius, whose position in Cyrene as a man of wealth and birth gave him especial prominence, perhaps, too, with the fame of his oratorical powers still fresh from the schools of Alexandria, was chosen, in spite of his youth, to undertake the mission and plead his country's cause before Arcadius.

* Amm. Marc. XXVIII., p. 377-9.

† Probably the Embassy was in the name of the whole Pentapolis, for Synesius speaks more than once of the success of his journey as bringing relief to *the towns*—doubtless the five cities of Pentapolis. Cf. *De Regno,* 32 c., περὶ ὧν αἰτοῦσιν ἀι πολῖις, and *De Insomn.*, 148 A.

‡ Cod. Theod., b. xii., t. xii.

It was thus in the year 397* A.D. that Synesius left Cyrene, not without a sigh for the quiet home he was quitting, not without forebodings as to the time of trial that lay before him.

It is obvious from many passages in his writings that he always looked back upon these years as a period of exile. In one of his hymns† he tells us of the labours and pangs he endured with tears, bearing on his shoulders the cares of his mother-land. He speaks of his struggles by day, of his couch wet with tears by night ; and how in his distress there was not a temple in Byzantium or Chalcedon in which he had not offered up prayers for the success of his cause.

Again in the passage from the *De Insomniis*‡ already referred to, he says : "Books and the chase sum up my "life, except when I undertook the embassy, and would that "I had never seen three years of my life so wasted."

Clearly the Emperor was difficult of access; for Synesius reproaches him in his speech with keeping shut up within doors as though he were in some beleaguered city ; seeing and hearing as little as possible of the outer world. And he complains bitterly that while a philosopher is looked at askance, and kept at a distance, the door is always open to some brainless favourite whose frivolity is his sole recommendation. Well may Synesius have burned with indignation as he lay on a

---

* This is the first date in Synesius' life which can be fixed with approximate certainty. Aurelian was Consul in the year of Synesius' return, 400 A.D. ; and we know from Synesius' own words that he spent three years in Constantinople. *De Insomn.*, 148, and H. III.

† H. III.

‡ Possibly it was during this period of depression that Synesius nearly yielded to the artifices of certain magicians, against whom he was divinely warned in a dream. *De Insomniis*, 148 A. The passage is interesting as showing that he had not wholly escaped, with all his rationalism, from the superstitions of his time, which, under the disguise of science and philosophy, were made the medium of a traffic in information from the other world.

thick Egyptian rug* at the palace doors day after day and still found no admission, much less an audience for his cause.

His time, however, was not wholly wasted. A man of his genial temperament could not be long without making friends, and Synesius certainly made some very valuable ones.

⸝ Paeonius† was among them, a man of education and influence, and to whom Synesius made a present of an astrolabe or plan of the heavens, accompanying the gift with a dissertation still extant. In this he alludes to the protection afforded by Paeonius against malicious rivals, the dogs who barked at him ; and in a later letter to Hypatia, he sends the document to her with the recommendation that the Pentapolis had gained much from this work and the gift which it had accompanied.

Equally important as a friend at Court was Aurelian,‡ afterwards Consul in 400 A.D., and thrice prefect of the Prætorian guard. It was in his honour that Synesius began the singular allegorical work *De Providentia*, to which we shall have to return. Two names of importance remain to be mentioned, Troilus the sophist, whose influence during the minority of Theodosius II. was considerable, and his friend, Anthemius, the tutor of the infant prince, and for seven years (408-415) the virtual ruler of the Eastern Empire.

At last, doubtless through the influence of Aurelian, the long expected audience was granted, and Synesius laid his case before the Emperor in full court, introducing the actual plea by an oration which has been preserved to us under the title of "περὶ βασιλείας." Before

---

* Ep. 61.
† Sermo ad P., 310 D.   Cf. Ep. 153, ad fin.
‡ Ep. 31.

considering the speech in detail, it will be well, however, to say a word or two as to the date of its delivery.

It has been sufficiently shown on Synesius' own evidence that these three years were spent in weary waiting; and we might fairly infer from this that the audience was deferred almost to the end of his stay. Druon* argues that such bold language as Synesius uses would have been impossible while the favourite Eutropius was in power. Now his fall took place in the autumn of 399. Add to this an allusion in the speech to disturbances among the Goths† which can hardly refer to anything but the revolt of Tribigild in the same year, and we can, with a fair amount of confidence, date the audience and the speech not earlier than 399 A.D.

The speech itself has won commendation from all historians for its fearless frankness, and for the strange contrast it offers to the studied eulogies so familiar to an absolute monarch. But the universal practice of ancient orators, in the days when newspaper reports were unknown, must not be forgotten. Probably not a speech of Demosthenes, certainly not a speech of Cicero was delivered as it actually stands. The custom implied no dishonesty: it was a recognized thing, and the necessary polish that had to be given to a work which was destined for posterity, involved the embellishment of many a period, the strengthening of many an epithet. The language of Synesius was probably, therefore, more measured than the extant work would lead us to believe; and without assuming for a moment, as has been done, that the speech was never actually delivered, allowance must be made for subsequent alterations, and the severer strictures of

---

* *Druon,* p. 135.

† *De Regno,* p. 22, ἀκροβολισμοί τινες ἤδη γίγνονται.

its philosophy must be modified to no small extent.*

The speech presents two aspects, a philosophical and a practical. Under the cloak of philosophy Synesius introduces a rather tedious and unedifying portrait of the Ideal King, following pedantically in the footsteps of Dio Chrysostom, for whose works and character he seems to have had a sincere admiration. The practical portion of the speech is much more interesting, and throws considerable light on the customs of the court and the history of the times.

(1)† He commences with an apology for the humble position of the State whose cause he pleads ; disclaims all intentions of flattery, and hopes that philosophy and plain speaking, so salutary for a young prince, will not be resented by his audience.

(2) Cyrene is only mentioned by the way. "Cyrene "sends me to crown your head with gold, your soul with "philosophy : a city of Hellas, an ancient and honoured "name, sung in many a lay by the poets of old, now poor, "dejected, and sorely in need of a king whose policy shall "not disgrace her old renown. It rests with you to do this, "and to earn a second crown‡ of gold from a grateful State. "These are days when men can speak their minds, when "truthful speech is counted real nobility. The teacher who "can mould the mind of a great ruler to noble ends is "thereby benefiting the subjects who own that ruler's "sway."

---

* Cf. Constant Martha, *Etudes Morales sur l'Antiquité*, p 312. Nous croyons donc que Synésius, de retour dans sa patrie, pour faire honneur à son ambassade et rendant compte à ses concitoyens, a mis après coup, dans un discours d'apparat, non pas seulement ce qu'il avait dit à la cour, mais encore ce qu'il en pensait.

† The numbers in parentheses refer to the marginal pages in Migne's Edition.

‡ Gibbon, Vol. II., p. 321.

(3) The opportunity for instructing Arcadius is too good to be lost, but, as he notices a flutter of surprise among the courtiers, Synesius once more deprecates all offence at his outspokenness. Then he dwells on the power of the Emperor for good, the vastness of his Empire, the almost superstitious awe with which he is regarded by distant cities and peoples, whom he has never seen, and who never hope to see him. Upon all this the Emperor is to be congratulated, but not praised. Congratulation is paid to outward prosperity, praise to innate merit. Arcadius, unlike his father, the great Theodosius, was born in the purple, and was indebted to fortune rather than to virtue for his high station. His father won the throne by his own exertions; the sons have succeeded to the inheritance for which they never toiled, and must fear the fickleness of fortune. Then follows the portraiture of the Ideal King.

(6) The true king is he who seeks always the good of his subjects, who is ready to sacrifice his own ease that he may save them trouble, and to meet their perils that they may live in security, to be watchful, to have care ever at his side that they may be saved from all anxieties by night and day: this is the true shepherd of his sheep—this is among men the true King.

Synesius gives the reverse of the picture, and then adds— This is the standard by which you must measure yourself. If you come up to it then you are worthy of your name; if not, try to mend your defects and grow in the likeness of what you ought to be. Youth is the time of promise, of strong impulses and passions, when the guiding hand of philosophy is doubly necessary.

(7) Virtue and vice are next door neighbours, and the transition from one to the other is easy. Thus it is that Tyranny and Kingship lie close together. For what is power but a potentiality of good or evil as the case may

be? And what turns the scale in the right direction but a well-regulated will? Wisdom therefore is the highest good, without which happiness and prosperity are nothing. Power is helpless without it. This is what the Egyptians symbolize in their two-faced Hermes, at once youth and sage; in the sphinx, half-beast half-human. The Emperor must ensure the possession of wisdom, and the other three great virtues will follow in her train.

(8) External goods, as defined by Plato and Aristotle, may serve the ends of vice as well as of virtue. A fool is less harmful in a humble station of life. He has fewer opportunities of realizing his mad schemes; the mischief he works is on a smaller scale. Let us pray then that power may fall into worthy hands; and let it be Arcadius' aim that all the peoples of the earth may bless his rule.

It is in imitating the providence of God, the Archetype of the world, that the true king is revealed. The earthly king must be the friend of the heavenly, unless he belies his name. Who can define the true nature of God? Man can only feel after him through his visible creation, and all the attributes of Divinity lead us back to what proceeds from God, and not to God himself.

(9) Various are his attributes; yet all agree in ascribing to him goodness, not absolute, but relative to us his people. God is the giver of what is good—life, and being, and reason. The Emperor must, after the divine example, scatter the blessings of prosperity among his subjects if he is to deserve the title of "Great."

To return to the Ideal Ruler, whom Arcadius is to contemplate and embody in his life. Let reverence be the sure basis on which our image shall stand unshaken by storms.

(10) Let the King first be king over himself; let reason be supreme in his mind, having overthrown the mob-rule of the passions.

(11) From this point begins the practical portion of the speech—the King in his aspect towards the outer world. His friends will be friends in the true sense of the term; they will share his successes and troubles; their praise will be sincere, their censure kindly. Their happiness is an evidence to his people of the King's goodness. They will supplement his judgment by wise counsel, and so multiply his force that he will see and hear with the eyes and ears of all.

(12) Lastly, flattery, the great danger of Royal friendships, must be avoided at all hazards.* No guards can keep it from the palace gates, but once it has gained an entrance it saps the very foundations of the kingly mind.

His soldiers form the second rank of the King's friends. The Emperor must frequent the camp, join in all warlike exercises, and make the term *commilitones* bear a new and real meaning. Soldiers are easily won by such treatment. Let them know their Emperor otherwise than by hearsay or from pictures.

(13) Even a knowledge of the names of his men is an advantage to the General (Agamemnon is represented in Homer as calling all his troops by name), and in any case he should be familiar with their ways and customs.

---

* Synesius might well warn the Emperor against the evil influence of favourites in a court. He naturally mentions no names, but he must have been thinking of the wretched Eutropius, who for four years practically ruled the empire. Gibbon (Vol. III., c. 32, p. 170) says—"Under the weakest of the "predecessors of Arcadius the reign of the eunuchs had been secret and "almost invisible. Eutropius was the first of his artificial sex who dared to "assume the character of a Roman magistrate and general." His venality and injustice brought misery to the inhabitants of the whole empire, for the provinces were shamelessly put up to auction in his antechamber and sold to the highest bidder. His rivals in power were removed by the hand of the assassin or the equally potent engine of false accusation, so that during his four years of office not only was the noblest blood shed by the executioner, but the most inhospitable extremities of the empire were filled with innocent and illustrious exiles.

(14) Nothing in the past has had such a pernicious influence on the empire as the absurd pomp and luxury that fence the person of the Emperor. Arcadius is not to be blamed for this—his predecessors rather. But the Emperor should be accessible and not fear lest familiarity should breed contempt. At present he lives as if in a beleaguered fortress, seeing and hearing as little as possible of the outside world—the life of a mollusc rather than of a man.

(15) Who find readiest access to his presence? Not the philosopher, but men of small mind, nature's base coins, hysterical jesters who pass the day in foolery. The language of such men is far more familiar to his ears than the divine truths of philosophy.

(16) Look at the institutions of your Roman forefathers, not at the luxurious fashions of to day. καί μοι πειρῶ διαμεῖναι, θυμοδακὴς γὰρ ὁ μῦθος. "When think you was "the Roman state more prosperous? Since you go clothed "in purple and gold? Since the precious stones sought "out from barbarous mountains and seas adorn your "heads, link your sandals and your cloaks, and form the "ornament of your girdles, so that you present a spectacle, "like peacocks, wondrous in diversity and brilliance of "colour and draw upon yourselves the Homeric curse of "the cloak of stones? Nay, even this tunic is not "enough for you. When you attain the office of consul, ."the assembly of your peers is closed to you, unless you "invest yourselves in another robe as gorgeous. And "those to whom a glimpse of you is vouchsafed, look up to "you among our senators, as if you alone were happy, "as if you alone bore the real labour of legislation. And "you are proud of your burden, like the captive in golden "fetters who forgot his misery and, cajoled by the magnifi- "cence of his bondage, thought no shame of his lot.

"The pavement and the bare earth are too hard for your
"delicate feet; your progress must be sprinkled with
"gold dust brought over land and sea from distant
"climes. . . . . Is it better so than in the days when
"our armies were led by generals who lived a soldier's
"life? Browned by the sun, plain to severity in their
"habits; breathing no dithyrambic airs of empty pride—
"they wore the woollen cap of Sparta, that the boys of
"to-day mock at upon their statues—until even the older
"generation begin to think that these heroes, far from
"being happy, were miserable in comparison with you.
"Yet they had no need to fortify their homes against
"the invasion of barbarians from Asia or from Europe.
"It was in their own achievements that they found the
"best rampart against the foe. . . . To-day, the very
"people they conquered, bring panic to your gates and
"demand tribute from you as the price of peace.—ἢν μὴ
"σύ γε δύσσεαι ἀλκήν."

(17) Synesius then contrasts the old frugality with the
luxury of his day, and in illustration he narrates the tale of
Carinus and the Parthian ambassadors. (18) He lays special
emphasis on the simple ways of the Emperor, the difficulty
of distinguishing him from his retinue, and the contrast
between his soldierly escort and the glittering bodyguard of Arcadius with their shields and spears of gold,
from whose approach men infer the Emperor's presence,
as it were the sun by his rays. The Parthians were at
a loss to recognise in the plainly clad general, the Ruler
of Rome, who was partaking of a frugal meal of salt
pork and peas, and invited them without ceremony to
join him. But when, taking off his helmet and pointing
to his bald head, he replied to their message in the
following terms: "Tell your young sovereign, that unless
"he comes to his senses, his kingdom shall be made barer

"than the head of Carinus," their surprise knew no bounds ; and their King on receiving the tidings of what they had seen, panic-stricken at an Emperor who dined at the same table with his officers and was not ashamed of his baldness, at once tendered his submission.

(19) The title of *Imperator*, the avoidance of the term *rex*, shows the innate hatred of tyranny in the Roman mind. Arcadius, therefore, to avoid the suspicion even of tyranny, must emulate the Divine power—for God reveals himself by no stage effects, nor by the working of wonders, but moving on his silent course guides with justice the affairs of men.

(20) All this points to the mistake of avoiding familiarity with one's people. We see the sun daily, but no man yet has despised it. Let the Sovereign therefore be κοινότατος. To make a practical application of the theory.

(21) The time is past for indolence and repose. The whole fate of the Empire rests on the turn of a die. God alone and a good ruler can avert the catastrophe.

(22) The soldiers are the watch-dogs, as Plato calls them, of the Empire, and the shepherd must take care that there be no wolves among them. Arms should only be given to the men who are born and reared in the country they protect, not to Scythians and aliens.* The latter course is simply to hang the stone of Tantalus over our own heads by a thread.† They will rise against you whenever they see their opportunity : already there are signs of the coming

* Note that Synesius always speaks of the Goths as Scythians, with his usual vagueness on historical questions. After the death of Athanaric in 382 A.D., the Goths, conquered but still formidable, were admitted into the Empire with the title of allies about 386 A.D. by Theodosius, who allotted to them Thrace and several provinces of Asia Minor to settle in.—Gibbon, Vol. II., c. xxvi., p. 504.

† Synesius is referring to some unknown legend of Tantalus : it is quite as likely, however, that his mythology is a little mixed, and he means the sword of Damocles.

storm. And the worst of all is that there is no force to
counterpoise theirs. We grant remission from service for
the asking to the very men who ought to be armed for the
defence of their country. The idle mob spend their time in
the theatres instead of in the field. It is in the family as in
the state—the man defends, the woman sees to her domestic
affairs in-doors. We are playing the woman's part.

(23) Let us mend matters before it is too late. The
Scythians must be excluded from magistracies, the office of
senator, and above all of general. What is more extraordinary than our inconsistency in this matter, these
Scythians are the people whose womanish cowardice
Herodotus makes scorn of. Our own eyes witness it.
Every household has its Scythian slaves, and yet the men
of this same race are fast filling all our offices. Remember
the revolt of Spartacus and the peril of Rome.

(25) We must treat them as the Lacedæmonians did the
Messenians, confine them to agriculture or send them back
to where they came from.* So far we have treated of the
King as warrior, now we must speak of him as civil
governor. The two functions are closely allied, for war is
or ought to be a means to peace. The Sovereign must mix
with his people more, as with his soldiers.

(27) The privilege of the provinces in their right of
appeal to the Emperor by embassy is a valuable one. It
rests with Arcadius to make it still more so. He owes a
debt to all his subjects equally, and in making access to his
presence easy, and in showing a gracious interest in their
grievances, he is only performing a duty. (i.) Let the
troops who are told off for defence deal fairly with the
citizens, who are their charge. (ii.) The tribute must not
be exhausting.

(28) To secure the latter reform, the prince must curtail

* v. note on p. 28.

his luxury. An age of luxury involves avarice as well as extravagance. Both are signs of a decaying state. Once more, the Sovereign, in this as in other matters, must set the example, and by assuring his people freedom from evils secure to them leisure for good works and the worship of the gods. There is no sight more to be revered than a Sovereign raising his hands among his people, and worshipping the King who is his Lord and theirs.

(30) The choice of magistrates should be more careful: ability not wealth ought to be the criterion. The Emperor should keep himself informed of the doings of the magistrates. As it is, a wealthy man buys the privilege and turns his administration into a source of gain.

(31) Let merit even in poverty be rewarded. The Ruler has only to set the fashion and his dependents will follow suit. Synesius prays that the Emperor may turn his attention to philosophy and true culture; in that event, Plato's dream may be realised, and Arcadius will be the Philosopher King.

Such in brief outline was the speech delivered by Synesius, and on the whole it justifies the epithet applied by our writer to himself, τῶν πώποτε Ἑλλήνων θαρραλεώτερον. The most striking feature about it is its hopeful tone. It is true that Synesius strikes boldly at the pomp and Eastern luxury of the Court, and at the unwise seclusion of the Emperor, but the language of indignation, the piteous outcry of Cyrene never once makes itself heard. The speaker seems so confident of the speedy reform of the evils he indicates, that the mere anticipation of redress has enabled him to cast off the burden of his troubles. To a later age, which must recognise the hopeless weakness of Arcadius, his utter incompetency to act for himself, or even to listen intelligently to the advice of wise counsellors, there seems

Character of the Speech.

something pathetic in the sanguine hopes of Synesius.

One notices too at times a quaint unpractical air, as when he recurs again and again to the Ideal King, and especially in the suggestion so characteristic of Alexandrine pedantry, that Arcadius might well imitate Agamemnon and know all his soldiers by their names. It has been suggested that he addresses the Emperor as though he were a Spartan King—a Spartan King would hardly have sat through so long an oration without bringing Synesius to the point at issue.

On the other hand there is a statesmanlike forethought in many of his proposals, and especially where he is speaking on the subject he knew best, the condition of the provinces. But while allowing him credit for appreciating the danger of the Goths* to the Empire, it is plain that he wholly failed to realise the rottenness of the existing system, the impossibility of preserving the tottering structure except by securing for its defence the new races that threatened its destruction. Gibbon's evidence† on this point is clear :—"The difficulty of levies increased yearly ; "no amount of donatives, no invention of new emoluments "and indulgences could compensate in the eyes of the "degenerate youth for the hardships and dangers of a "military life. And though the rigour of conscription was "occasionally exercised in the provinces, and every "proprietor was obliged either to take up arms or to "procure a substitute, or to purchase his exemption by a "heavy fine, the sum of forty-two pieces of gold, to which "it was *reduced,* ascertains the exorbitant price of volunteers

---

* Synesius was misled by his contempt for the Gothic character at this period, and underestimated their courage.—*De Regno,* 23, 24. In *The Dion,* p. 46, he is fairer to them, and concedes to the barbarian a superiority over the Greek in dogged courage and tenacity of purpose.

† Gibbon, Vol. II., c. xvii., p. 38.

"and the reluctance with which the government admitted
"of this alternative."

In view of facts like these, Synesius' idea that the city
mob might be turned to account and made to serve in the
army is obviously absurd. The only means of maintaining
the very existence of the army was the admission into its
ranks of the hardy nations of the north.

One other work of importance was the fruit of the
three years' stay at Constantinople—the first part of the
De Providentia; and as it deals so exclusively with the
course of events that followed almost immediately on the
close of the year 399, it will be well to give a short sketch
of the thrilling events of the succeeding year before dealing
with the historical aspect of the work in question.

In the very year in which Synesius delivered his speech, *Course of events from 397 to 400. Historical Introd. to De Providentia.*
the revolt of Tribigild, the Goth, in Asia Minor, shook the
outward security of the empire. Gainas, also a Goth, was
commissioned by Eutropius to crush the rebellion, and after
playing into the hands of Tribigild for some time, at length
declined, on the pretext of inability, to prosecute the war,
and, insisting on the need of negotiation with Tribigild,
demanded through him the death of Eutropius. Eutropius
was saved for the time by the eloquence of Chrysostom,
and Synesius may have been present at that impressive
scene, when the Archbishop, ascending the pulpit of the
Cathedral, pleaded for the wretch as he lay crouching by
the altar.

While the fate of Eutropius however was being decided,
Gainas openly revolted; the Emperor was compelled to
come to terms, and Constantinople was filled with the Goths
who soon showed inclinations to pillage. A sudden out-
burst of popular energy, seconded by the palace guards,
saved the city. The gates were closed and seven thousand
of the barbarians massacred. Fravitta, a Gothic leader,

and a confederate of Gainas, deserted to the Imperial cause and the discomfiture of the Goths was complete. An attempt to force the passage of the Hellespont was intercepted, and eleven days after, the head of Gainas was brought to Constantinople.

Synesius was a spectator throughout of these stormy scenes, and seems to have had his doubts as to the government of the world by an all-seeing Power. At any rate some theory to account for the presence of evil and its apparent or even actual triumph in the darker epochs of history was needed, and this want the *De Providentia* attempts to supply. It was finished after the return of the ἄριστοι (Aurelian and his party), and was written at their request.

The Narrative of the *De Providentia* in its historical connection.

Synesius himself styles this work a μῦθος, and in his remark that perhaps it may hint at something beyond the mythical, he clearly indicates the blending of fact with fiction, which in the second part of the work is so thinly disguised, that passages of it may almost be called historical. The scene is laid in Egypt, and there under the names of Osiris and Typho, he personifies the struggle between the powers of good and evil for the mastery of the world.

That Osiris represents Aurelian is generally admitted, but the majority of writers on this subject have hesitated to identify Typho with Gainas, and have found themselves driven to form absurd hypotheses; as for example, that Aurelian had a wicked brother who was his evil genius and thwarted all his efforts for good. The real truth seems to be that Typho represents vaguely, the evil influences that were sapping the foundations of the empire. In some passages he is clearly not Gainas; for instance, on p. 109, the Scythian leader is to supply the men, and Typho lends the patronage of his name.

Again the descriptions of the wife of Typho as, διωλύγιον κακὸν, ἐαυτῆς κομμωτρίαν, with her insatiate appetite for shows and the theatre, point to a wider interpretation of Typho and his wife as the embodiment of the corrupt tendencies of the time.

On the other hand, in p. 115, the demand of the heretical sect for a temple of their own, is an obvious allusion to Gainas and his Arian followers. But the end of Typho, in p. 123, is not consistent with what we know of the death of Gainas. The wider interpretation, therefore, seems distinctly preferable, and it has the advantage of dispensing with any fanciful hypothesis as to the real person intended, if such there be. I cannot agree, therefore, with Druon on this point, who says: "A notre sens, "Gaïnas est donc encore plus nettement indiqué que ne " l'est Aurélien lui-même."

Osiris and Typho are two princes, sons of a King of Thebes. But with widely different inclinations and temperament, they gave early indication of their future development. (90) Osiris was noted for his thirst after knowledge, his quiet, modest ways, his deference to elders, and his charity towards mankind in general which made him constantly prefer the petitions of suppliants to his father. Typho hated all wisdom, mocked at his teachers, and set his brother's quiet decent behaviour down to timidity instead of modesty. (91) As for himself he gorged and slept, and thought bodily strength the highest of all goods. As they grew up and took part in the government, the contrast became still more marked; Osiris distinguished himself by his virtues, and his fairness and justice made him the idol of all good citizens. Typho by abandoning himself to every kind of vice and dissipation won only the esteem of companions as worthless as himself. (93) The time came, however, for

Abstract of the Narrative.

the choice of a sovereign, and Osiris won the unanimous
support of gods and men. The rage of Typho knew no
bounds, and there is a fine description of the agonies of
his jealousy and wounded pride. (104) Osiris, however,
though warned by God and his most faithful counsellors to
banish his brother and incapacitate him for further evil,
prefers to rely on the Divine providence, and tries from
mistaken motives to overcome evil by good. (105) But
Typho, aided and urged on by his wife who is more worthless even than himself, and maintains her ascendency over
him by the vilest practices, enters into a secret conspiracy
with the alien bands of the soldiery who are quartered
in Egypt. And by the false assertion that Osiris was
planning the extermination of the Scythians, he wins them
over to his views. (108) By their aid he overthrows the
Government. The Scythian leader, who is not nearly so
depraved as his tempter, spares the life of Osiris against
the will of Typho, and sends him into exile to the distress
of his disconsolate subjects. The second act in the drama,
records the miraculous deliverance of the city from the
Scythians. (118) Already depredations had commenced, and
the flight or exile of the wealthier citizens was becoming
general, when an old beggar woman, who stood at
the gates of the city, was cut down by a Scythian of
whom she asked an alms. Her death was at once
avenged by an Egyptian, and the fight became general.
(121) The people of their own motion, without generals,
but with some divine impulse to inspire them, won
an easy victory, and after a massacre of the Scythians,
held an assembly and recalled Osiris from banishment,
who reigned from that time undisturbed upon his throne
after pardoning once more the unworthy Typho.

The question naturally arises—Where was Synesius
during these days? Did he share the exile of his friends

or stay in the city? The Second Part of the *De Providentia*, which is obviously the work of an eye-witness, bears out the latter alternative; and if, as is almost certain, we may safely identify with Synesius himself the philosopher of rustic and simple ways who figures at the close of Part I., pp. 113, 114, we have definite information as to his behaviour in the captured city. And indeed this personage, who owes to Osiris exemption from public charges, and who has procured for his fellow citizens the alleviation of their taxes; this poet, who sings the praises of his patron in Dorian measures, must be the writer himself and no other.

It would seem then that he not only upheld before the people the falling cause of Aurelian by his eloquence, but dared to pronounce his eulogy in the presence even of Gainas himself. There is no hint, it is true, of this event in any other of Synesius' writings; the circumstances of the fact, if it be such, are wholly unknown, but it is difficult to believe that Synesius is romancing in this matter.

The result of his mission was on the whole satisfactory, *Result of the Mission.* if we may judge from Synesius' allusions to its success on more than one occasion.* He thanks God that his country had through his means found delivery from the miseries that overwhelmed her. He pays a tribute too to Troïlus, who doubtless assisted him in his solicitation; it is to him, he says in one of his letters, that Cyrene owes her existence as a city still.

At the time, however, he may well have had grave doubts on the question; the revolt of Gainas had threatened the ruin of the empire, and affairs must still have been in a precarious state when Synesius quitted Constantinople suddenly in the year 400. He departed without bidding *Sudden departure for* farewell to his friends, even to Aurelian.† The cause of this *Cyrene.*

* H. III., 470-480.
† Ep. 61, 204.

C

haste was an earthquake which drove all the people into the streets and squares, and made prayer fashionable for a time. " For myself," says Synesius, " I concluded that the "sea would be safer than the land, and so hurried on board " my ship and set sail without a word to anyone."

Influence of these three years on Synesius' character.
It only remains to discuss the influence of these three years upon Synesius' life and character. In many ways it was a time of trial, and thus a strengthening influence. He must have seen the hopeless corruption of the government, and have realised the necessity of self-reliance for the provinces. Perhaps the full consciousness of this truth did not come home to him till that later time when Cyrene seemed lost beyond recovery ; and he may have thought when he wrote the *De Providentia* that the dark shadow which seemed to be drawing in on every side would lift after a time, and that the return of Osiris would bring peace and prosperity to a weary world. However this may have been, the strange and rapid succession of events, the almost miraculous delivery of Constantinople from the Goths, must have set Synesius thinking on the Divine Economy and the deeper questions of life.

Possible leanings to Christianity.
We are certainly not warranted in assuming his conversion to date from this period, but it is extremely probable that he felt drawn towards Christianity, and in any case the impression made upon his mind during so long a stay in a Christian city must count for something. He must have heard Chrysostom denounce with burning eloquence the vanities of the Court. He must have felt the reality of the influence which the Church exercised more widely every year: and what more natural to a philosophic mind than to enquire into the secret of that influence?

We know from the third hymn that he visited the Churches in his distress and offered prayers to God. These may have been, probably were, simply the aspirations of a

Neo-Platonist, his endeavour after ecstatic union with the
Supreme Being. But the fact that he paid his devotions in
Churches dedicated to the service of the New Religion,
shows that he must have been somewhat attracted by it
—for the philosopher was surely independent of temples
made by hands, and needed no popular ritual to aid his
aspirations; nay, was rather out of sympathy as a philosopher with any such place or ceremony. Without pressing
therefore the fact as recorded by Synesius, we may fairly
assume distinct leanings to the prevalent religion, and we
would adduce in further confirmation of the assumption two
passages from the speech *De Regno*.

In the first* he says, speaking of the attributes of God,
" and the sacred prayers at the solemn rites send forth the
" cry, ' Our Father ' to the God who is over all, not glorifying
" his power but reverencing his providence." The second†
has been already quoted : " There is no sight more to be
" revered than that of a Sovereign raising his hands in
" prayer before his people, and worshipping the King who is
" his Lord and theirs."

The first passage, by its conception of God's fatherhood
to us his people, by its allusion to the sacred prayers and
solemn mysteries, may point to a realization of the spiritual
power of what was at Constantinople the one religion ; the
second passage indicates a certain love of ritual, an
appreciation of such majestic ceremony as Synesius may
have often witnessed in the Imperial city.

* *De Regno*, p. 9. Adopting the emendation of Camerarius, πάτερ ἡμων for
πατέρων ἡμῶν, the reading of the text, against which it may fairly be objected
that it is not usual Greek for "of our fathers," and secondly that it leaves
ἐκβοῶσαι without an object. Too much stress, however, must not be laid on
the passage : For the assumption that " Our Father " is a reminiscence of the
Lord's Prayer, and that the solemn rites represent the Sacrament of the Last
Supper, would lead to the conclusion that Synesius was already converted,
when he certainly was not. The words must be taken generally ; the reference
to the rites need not be pressed, nor the notion of God's fatherhood to man
confined to Christian doctrine.

† *De Regno*, p. 29.

CYRENE AND ALEXANDRIA.

400—409 A.D.

RETURN TO CYRENE.

SYNESIUS found Cyrene in sad plight upon his return in
400. The barbarians, Ausurians and Macetae, emboldened
by success were ravaging the country on all sides. They
were powerless against regular troops, and a small force by
showing a firm front would have made short work of the
brigands; but either all troops had been withdrawn from the
country districts, or the old policy of inaction was again in
force, aggravated probably by the conflicting interests of
military and civil rule.*

Synesius was himself of opinion† that the best thing for
Cyrene would have been the abolition of the local *imperium*,
by which arrangement the province would have come under
the immediate control of the Prefect of Egypt. But his
proposal was rejected on grounds of private interest. He
asks bitterly in another letter,‡ "why is it that Phoenicians
"do not rule Phoenicians, nor Coelosyrians Coelosyrians,
"and the Egyptians any province rather than their own,
"while the Libyans are left to govern themselves?" Whatever the cause, however, nothing could have been worse
than the state of the country. In a letter to Hypatia,||
written at this time, he speaks of the enemy as daily in

Distress at
Cyrene.

Evils of Local
Government.

* Gibbon, Vol. II., C. xvii., p. 35, describes the separation by Constantine,
throughout the provinces, of the military and civil administration—a measure
which "relaxed the rigour of the State, while it secured the tranquillity of the
"monarch."

† Ep. 94. 235 C.

‡ Ep. 73. 220 B.

|| Ep. 124.

sight. The very air is tainted with the bodies of the slain. And he asks, "how can one cherish hope under a sky "darkened by the clouds of carrion-birds that await their "horrid meal?" Still he will be faithful—"Am I not a "Libyan, born here and with the tombs of my ancestors "ever before my eyes?" But Synesius was not the man to rest content with idle lamentations: he roused himself to meet the occasion, and exhorted his fellow-citizens to seek a remedy in themselves.* "What!" he asks, "while these "robbers brave death so lightly, rather than give up. the "spoils they have wrested from us, are we to shrink from "danger when the safety of our hearths, our altars, our laws, "our fortunes, is at stake? We must march against these "barbarians, and if we only fight as if we cared nothing for "death, we shall conquer and survive. I am a descendant "of Sparta, and I recall the words of the Ephors to "Leonidas: 'Let the soldiers go into battle as if they were "'doomed to perish, and they will not perish.'"

It is a relief after this tragic language to come across a more humorous episode, which caused much diversion on the occasion of one of these barbarian raids.† A certain John, a Phrygian by birth, a Commander of Horse by profession, and a boastful coward to boot, was nowhere to be found when a rumour of the enemy's approach spread abroad. Synesius describes the march out into the open plain, and the waiting for the foe. At evening the troops returned after an agreement to meet for the same purpose the next day—all this time the Phrygian John was nowhere to be seen. A report however was spread that he had broken his leg, and was suffering from asthma; but where he was remained as great a mystery as ever. In the night the enemy withdrew into the skirts of the province; and

Episode of John, the Phrygian.

* Ep. 113.
† Ep. 104.

when on the fifth day they failed to come up with them, the valiant John suddenly appeared, to the astonishment of all, and, ridiculing the idea of his having been ill in any way, explained that he had just arrived from some place or other at a distance. His present intention, he said, was to make with all speed for the scene of danger; and he thought that if his presence were not betrayed, the enemy might be emboldened to attack us. Evening drew on once more, and the hour of attack was approaching when a group of four youths, country lads, came galloping towards us, with heads strained forward to shout. It needed no oracle to inform us that the enemy was on their rear, and in a few moments, before they actually came up with us, we espied their pursuers, poor thin little men on horseback, with a half-starved look, as though they were ready to die to secure our goods. Before they came within range, however, they dismounted and prepared for battle after their fashion. I bade my men do likewise, as the ground was unsuited for cavalry manœuvres. The brave John, however, was not going to dismount, he was for fighting on horseback: and the next we saw of him he was galloping full speed in the opposite direction, with loose rein, spurs going, and clearing the most astounding obstacles in his course. When last we heard of him, he was safe in the seclusion of some rock fastness at Bombaea—but his bullying days are over, and he will swagger in the forum no more.

The barbarians were never finally repulsed. But a period of comparative peace must have been secured to the unhappy Pentapolis, for on no other theory can we explain the opportunities for study and retirement which Synesius seems to have enjoyed in the intervals between these raids into the desert, during the few years that elapsed between his return from Constantinople and his second visit to Alexandria.

Adventure on voyage from Alexandria to Cyrene.

To this period possibly belongs the adventure, so graphically described in the fourth letter. He took ship from Alexandria to Cyrene, and on the way they were driven by a gale far out to sea. The pilot was a strict Jew, and at the most critical moment of the storm on Friday evening, left the rudder and refused to break his sabbath by steering the ship. It was not till towards midnight, when they seemed on the point of sinking, that the Jew, remarking that the law permitted him to work now they were in actual danger, returned to the helm. The next morning they landed on a strange coast, and were hospitably entertained by the barbarous inhabitants until they could start for home again.*

Synesius' country life.

Synesius was not rich, but he had a sufficient income for the needs of a philosopher and his friends.† And he seems to have retired to his farm, relieving, like Xenophon, the study of philosophy with the pursuits of agriculture and the excitements of the chase. He sums his life up in the words βίβλοι καὶ θηρά;‡ and again, he says " my fingers are more used to handle the mattock " than the pen."‖

For with all his Neo-Platonic mysticism, his craving for the life of pure contemplation, Synesius was thoroughly sane and healthy in his view of life. Man, he admits, cannot always be bent on meditation.§ The Ascetics

---

* There is a vexed point of chronology connected with this letter. The theory of Petavius, based on a lunar observation, would place the date of this event on Wednesday, 14th Sept., 410. Tillemont, however (Vol. XII., p. 686-7), establishes Tuesday as the day of the new moon mentioned in the letter and so explodes the theory. Druon, p. 275, follows Tillemont, and of the alternative years which would suit the day in question, 396 or 402 A.D., prefers the former.

† Ep. 133.

‡ *De Insomniis*, 148.

‖ *Calv. Encomium*, p. 66 D.

§ *Dion*, 46 D.

in the desert are driven to occupy their time with basket-
weaving. What better alternative then than a cultured
life with harmless pleasures such as the country best
affords? Surely men may be driven by ennui to worse
devices, ἃ μηδὲ εἰπεῖν ἄξιον.*

History is full of strange contrasts: but none are more
striking, more cheering than the glimpses of quiet happiness
and of peaceful life that one catches through the gloom
even of the darkest ages. A letter, a chapter in a biography,
often preserved by the merest chance, reveals a period to us
in a new light and comes across the centuries like a breath
of fresh air, to strengthen and reassure.

Here is a letter from Synesius to his brother, then lying
ill at Phycus, a port on the Cyrenaic sea-board. He invites
him to come and breathe a purer atmosphere :—" Do you
" wonder at your chills and poor blood, if you will live in that
" sultry Phycus? It would be far more surprising if your
" physique held out against such a climate. But if you will
" only pay me a visit, by God's help there is a chance of
" your being set up when you are once out of air tainted with
" marsh vapours, and have left behind you the tepid salt
" lagoons, lying so stagnant you might call them dead. What
" charm is there in sitting on the sand of the sea-shore, your
" only haunt, for where else can you turn? But here you
" may creep under the shade of some tree, and, if it likes
" you not, pass from tree to tree ; nay from grove to grove,
" leaping across the stream that runs prattling by. How
" delightful the breeze that stirs the boughs so gently!
" Here is the changeful song of birds, the bright hues of
" flowers, the bushes in the meadows. Side by side are the
" works of man's hand and the free gifts of nature. The air
" is laden with perfumes, the earth rich with generous juices.
" And this grotto, fit home for the nymphs—I will spare it

* *Dion,* 45.

"my praises, for it needs a Theocritus to sing it as it
"deserves."*

Such was the home in which Synesius, during the
intervals of war and absence, spent what he always looked
back upon afterwards as the happiest years of his life. He
may have felt lonely at times, but solitude,† he says, is the
best handmaid of philosophy ; and in the same letter he
tells how he fancied sometimes that the very stars looked
down with kindly influence upon the one human being in
that region who could look up to them with the eyes of
knowledge.‡ And it must have been on some such
occasion that he spent a sleepless night gazing on the
mystery of the heavens.|| There is little doubt that much
of Synesius' religious poetry was the outcome of this period
of spiritual self-communion. But this question will be
discussed more fully when we come to treat of the hymns.
That he did write more or less between 400 and the year of
his visit to Alexandria is clear. The *Cynegetica*, a poem on
hunting, to which he alludes§ disparagingly in one of his
letters, and which has not come down to us, belongs to this
period : but we do not need its evidence to prove his
passion for hunting.

He mentions his dogs as a worthy theme for song,¶
"who fear not hyænas and strangle wolves." The hunts-
man too deserves his meed of praise for securing peace
and safety to the fields. He dreams of hunting by night,**
and one of the pleas he urges against accepting the
office of bishop, is that he cannot bear the thought of

* Ep. 114.
† Ep. 100, 239 D.
‡ H. II., 23-30.
|| *Catas.*, p. 303 C.
§ Ep. 100.
¶ Ep. 147.
** *De Insomn.*, 148 B.

seeing his dogs idle and his bow worm-eaten.* He was a kind master and indulgent to his slaves, most of whom sooner or later acquired their freedom.† But perhaps the best picture of his life at this period, and of his pleasant intercourse with the simple country-folk, is given in the long chatty letter to Olympius,‡ which must have been written in one of the intervals of peace between the barbarian inroads.

He talks at some length about the natural products of the country and in describing the innocence of the country people, he tells us how they shook their heads at his stories of fish and started back in horror from a jar of Egyptian salt-fish, thinking them some new species of reptile, and the oldest and wisest of his audience still remained incredulous as to salt-water producing anything good or wholesome, when the best drinking fountains only harboured frogs and leeches. To these amiable rustics, the Emperor and his court were a kind of far-off dream. The existence even of the Emperor might have been doubted but for the mundane and regular appearance of the tax-gatherer, a very real embodiment of the governing power. There were not a few who thought the Emperor was one and the same with a certain Agamemnon who sailed to Troy; and they had a great fondness for the adventures of one Ulysses, whom they looked upon as a contemporary hero. After all due allowance for playful exaggeration, the life of Synesius at this time, must have been, to use his own words, such as men lived in the days of Noe, before justice became a bond-slave.

While thus withdrawing himself from the life of cities, Synesius never forgot his duty to his friends or to his

* Ep. 105.
† *Dion.,* 59 D.
‡ Ep. 147.

country.* The man whom Hypatia speaks of as ἀλλότριον
ἀγαθόν,† was not likely to become a mere recluse, and
we find him constantly writing letters of introduction,
for fellow-citizens to his influential friends at Constantinople and Alexandria. In his own household he treated
his servants with consideration, and was rewarded by their
attachment and respect.‡

As for his friends his letters teem with expressions of
endearment. He writes, " Synesius, as long as he lives, will
" never fail to serve his friends with all his heart in every
" possible way."‖ Often he sends them presents, the
produce of his farm, or a horse reared by himself, or some
rare beast he has captured in hunting.§

Still this idyllic life was only to be enjoyed in snatches,
and the stately festival to which he compares it was rudely
interrupted at times.¶ He seems to have made enemies, as
was only natural after the exposure of the incompetence
of the ruling powers, and the contrast of his own address
and courage. That these men made his life wretched at
times is plain from his letters, and probably led to his
He leaves departure for Alexandria in the year 403 A.D. He writes
Cyrene for
Alexandria. from there, " I count myself happy to have escaped from
" friends and enemies of that description. I wish to remain
" at a distance, and have no more to do with them."**

In another letter he deplores the fate of Cyrene, once
the home of Carneades and Aristippus, but now abandoned
to such people as John and Julius, in whose society he

---

* οὐ μὴν διὰ τοῦτο ἀνθρώποις ἀσυντελῆ με πεποίηκεν ὁ Θεός, ἀλλὰ
πόλλακις ἡμῖν καὶ ἰδιῶται καὶ πόλεις εἰς δέον ἐχρήσαντο.

† Ep. 80.

‡ Ep. 32 and 144.

‖ Ep. 44.

§ Epp. 96, 133, 11, 129.

¶ Ep. 57.

** Ep. 50.

cannot live. What wonder then that such a state of affairs damped even the patriotism of Synesius, and made him long for the sight of his friends in Alexandria.

It was thus towards the commencement of the year 403* that Synesius took his departure for Egypt. He would find Hypatia still there, and their friendship must have been renewed and strengthened. But the two years spent at Alexandria are chiefly important from his intimacy with Theophilus, and the marriage of Synesius by that prelate's hand. It is difficult to understand the relations between these two men, so radically opposed in nature.

Intimacy with Theophilus.

Theophilus was a man of great force of character, but interest and ambition were the guiding principles of his life. He is in fact a fairly typical representative of the ecclesiastics, who by their strifes and jealousies brought the Eastern Church to a premature decay. He is accused of avarice, which may be scandal merely, but all writers are agreed as to his jealousy and the vindictive determination with which he pursued his rivals.

Character of Theophilus.

The best illustration, however, of his unscrupulous conduct is to be found in the treatment of the "Long Brothers" which led indirectly to the breach with Chrysostom.† A violent strife had arisen between the monks of the desert who held the grossest anthropomorphic notions as to the nature of the deity, and Theophilus who denied that God could have a material body. They even threatened him with death, and to elude their violence, Theophilus made an ambiguous reply: "In seeing you," he said, "I see the face of God"

* From Ep. 123 it appears that Synesius stayed two years in Alexandria, and that on his return he found Cyrene besieged. This siege took place in the year of Aristaenetus' Consulship (Ep. 132), *i.e.*, in 405, the commencement of the seven years' misfortune which Synesius speaks of in his *Catastasis*, p. 299, D, which was written in 412. *Druon*, p. 31.

† Socrates, VI., 7.

[οὕτως ὑμᾶς εἶδον ὡς Θεοῦ πρόσωπον]—implying his adherence to their views. He consented further to anathematise the works of Origen at their demand.

As a still more diplomatic stroke, he secured the services of the Long Brothers, who were the most prominent among the ascetics, and whose ability recommended them to his ambition. For a time all went well. Dioscorus, one of the four, was constrained to fill the see of Hermopolis; and the other brothers worked amicably with Theophilus.

They soon, however, found out the prelate's real character, and disgusted with his mercenary aims expressed a desire to return to the desert. Theophilus tried to dissuade them for a time, until he found out their real reason, whereupon he vowed vengeance; and knowing that with the monks on their side he could do nothing against them, he spread a malicious report that the brothers held the doctrine of Origen and denied bodily form to the Deity. The monks, most of them illiterate, violent men, with a few honourable exceptions turned upon the brothers, and Theophilus actually furnishing their enemies with arms, the four had to flee the country for their lives and took refuge at Constantinople.*

Chrysostom received them kindly (ἐν τιμῇ μὲν ἦγε τοὺς ἄνδρας); he withheld, however, the full rights of Churchmen until the matter had been satisfactorily cleared up. But a false report of his having received them into full communion reaching Theophilus' ears, the feud began which ended in the disgraceful victory of Theophilus and the deposition and exile of Chrysostom.†

Such was the man who seems to have won the friendship and respect of Synesius: a friendship which

* Socrates, VI., 9.
† Ibid., VI., 18.

some, in view of the real nature of Theophilus, have stigmatised as feigned. But such a supposition is wholly inconsistent with what we know of Synesius, and the clue to the mystery is to be found in his rather easy-going, good-natured temperament, which would not make him over ready to listen to the voice of scandal, or sound the truth of tales which did not redound to the credit of his friend.

Theophilus, on his side, like many men of overbearing nature, could doubtless make himself agreeable and genial enough to a man who was not likely to thwart his projects or rival his influence, and who had many interests and pursuits in common with his own. Here undoubtedly was the common ground on which they met. Theophilus was a man of considerable philosophic and scientific attainments, worthily maintaining in this respect the traditions of the Alexandrine Church ; and he was especially interested in astronomy, a science that we know to have been a favourite one with Synesius.

So much for their friendship. To deal next with its First steps to consequences. It seems highly probable that the first conversion date from this germs of Christianity, the first beginnings of a more intimate period. acquaintance with the articles of the Christian faith, were due to this intercourse between the prelate and Synesius.

In any case Synesius must have been a member of the Church before his consecration in 410.* It is impossible otherwise that he could have been even elected Bishop of Ptolemais. Now from the time of his leaving Alexandria, to that date, Cyrene was the scene of constant war, in which Synesius took an active part, and it seems very probable that his conversion had potentially begun during his stay at

---

* Moreover, in his letter (105) of protestation, he never suggests so obvious a disqualification as the fact of his not being baptized : nor is the statement of Evagrius, who fixes his baptism at the time of his consecration as bishop, sufficiently trustworthy to upset this theory.

D

Alexandria, while he was on intimate terms with the Archbishop and more or less under the ascendancy of his influence.

The objection so often raised, that his writings during this period show little trace of Christian influence, is not an adequate refutation of this view. The subject of the works was philosophic and they are dedicated to Hypatia—but surely an English theologian of scientific leanings might write a work on some technical subject and dedicate it, say, to Professor Huxley, without letting it appear on the surface that he was a theologian, and it would be much more absurd to expect that a man who had been brought up in the tenets of Neo-Platonism should at once abandon his old doctrines, or make any immediate parade of what was perhaps only a tendency towards a new belief.

Marriage of Synesius to a Christian wife. The fact remains, and facts are after all more important than theories, that Synesius was married by Theophilus.* Marriages between heathens and Christians were not uncommon at this period, though the Church generally looked askance upon such unions. But one inference is clear, that if Synesius was not converted, his wife was a Christian; and though in his letters we rarely find any mention of her, we may gather from these scanty allusions† that his affection for her was deep and real, and her influence in proportion considerable.‡

Assuming, therefore, that the work of conversion was

---

* It has been suggested that the language of Synesius need not mean more than that Theophilus was the means of bringing about his marriage. But the mention of the "sacred hand" of Theophilus, and the addition of the words "God and the law," seems to be conclusive against this interpretation. Vide Ep. 105.

† Ep. 105. H. VIII., 34.

‡ It is too much to infer from the passage in *De Provid.*, 105, that Synesius shared in the degraded Greek ideas of woman's place in society. "Osiris held that a woman's duty was never to be seen or heard of outside her own door." Cf. *Thuc.* II., c. 45.

begun at this time by Theophilus, it requires no great stress of imagination to see in the intercourse of a Christian wife and the slow work of time, ample causes for Synesius' gradual approximation to the Church. It is perhaps worth while to notice the contrast between the great city and the simple life of the country-folk among whom Synesius' lot was cast. Hypatia might well remain a Platonist in Alexandria, with its rich dilettante coteries, its brutal mob, and unscrupulous prelate. May not Synesius have seen a better side of Christianity in his native town—in the midst of a people tried and purified by the chastening of misfortune?

To this period belongs *The Dion*, an *Apologia pro vita* Writings of *sua*. It was written in the first year of his married life, and this period. is dedicated to the son whose birth was then expected. He sends it to Hypatia, with a letter, from which we learn that it was a reply to the criticisms of certain detractors who had reproached him with dilettanteism and a sophistical affectation of style. Synesius replies by giving the history of his mental development, and demonstrates the necessary connection of philosophy and letters.

After two years' sojourn at Alexandria, Synesius, at the Return to commencement of the year 405* returned to Cyrene, and Cyrene. found the country in a worse state than usual. Cerealius, the Governor of Pentapolis, was avaricious and cowardly. Instead of relieving the wretched towns, he wrung money from them, and used the scanty forces at his command for oppressing the citizens whom it was his duty to defend.

Naturally the Macetae and the other savage tribes availed themselves of the opportunity, and not content with ravaging the country districts, actually held Cyrene in a state of siege. Cerealius pursued a policy of masterly in-

* V. note † on p. 47.

action, embarked on board a vessel with as much portable property as he could take with him, and charging the Cyrenians not to engage the enemy, prepared for his own flight on the earliest opportunity.

The inhabitants finding that they must help themselves or perish made a stout defence, and Synesius took an active part in the labours of the siege. He served his turn on watch, devised engines of defence, and when the tide began to turn organized sorties against the barbarians. Cyrene was thus saved, but the war dragged on ; there was always fighting to be done, and Synesius was always ready to sacrifice his ease and his pursuits in the public cause.

He complains naturally of the inefficiency of the Government which so shamefully neglected its responsibilities. "We support troops," he says, "but it is we who defend ourselves, not they."* Everything depended on individual effort and Synesius was ably supported at times. He gives a glowing account in one of his letters† of the Deacon Faustus who marched unarmed at the head of the peasants of his valley and completely routed a band of the marauders. The incident is interesting not only from the gallant conduct of the brave Faustus, but also as showing how easily these barbarians might have been quelled by an organized attack of regular troops.

Of Synesius' private life during this period there is little to tell—two more sons were born to him, and he speaks of educating them at home, with his nephew Dioscuros. It has been remarked that there were intervals of peace in these troubled times, and it might have seemed that when

* Ep. 125.
† Ep. 122.

at last a lull in the invasions of the enemy was probable,
Synesius might have enjoyed the quiet happiness of his
home, and have spent his remaining days in the studies and
pursuits he loved so well.*   But it was otherwise ordained :
a new career awaited him.

* Ep. 57, 194, καὶ ἕζων μετ' ἀγαθῶν τῶν ἐλπίδων, ὥσπερ ἐν ἱερῷ περιβόλῳ
τῷ κόσμῳ, ζῷον ἄφετον, ἀνειμένον, εὐχῇ καὶ βίβλῳ καὶ θήρᾳ μερίζων τὸν βίον.

'οὐκ ἐπιλείψουσι στρατιῶται τῷ Θεῷ πρέποντες Ἐκκλησίαις."

Ep. 5.

SYNESIUS,

BISHOP OF PTOLEMAIS.

410—413. (?)

SYNESIUS CHOSEN BISHOP OF PTOLEMAIS.

IN the year 409 the Bishop of Ptolemais died and the see became vacant. The election rested with the people, the consecration of their choice with Theophilus, the patriarch of Alexandria. The office of Bishop involved a variety of duties—it was in fact a civil as well as a religious function—and the head of the church might be called upon to defend the material interests of his flock no less naturally than to promote their spiritual welfare.* It was not strange then that a feeling of gratitude and respect urged the people whom he had championed so unselfishly to choose Synesius as their pastor.

We have touched already on the vexed question of the date of his conversion, but whenever it may have taken place, it must clearly have preceded his election, though there are indications not a few of his imperfect acceptance, at that time, of the Christian religion. *(Was he a Christian at this time?)*

---

* It must be remembered in connection with Synesius' appointment, that the people required a man of some worldly ability. It was a necessity in those troubled times that the head of the Church should be ready for every emergency. to excommunicate a tyrannical governor, or to head a sally against a barbarian raid.

The case of Siderius, Bishop of Palaebisca, is singularly in point. The Metropolitan of the district, Orion, was old and feeble, and the inhabitants of Palaebisca, without waiting for his death, elected Siderius who was young and capable, had seen active service in the army of Valens and was a man to trouble his enemies and be of use to his friends. His election was wholly illegal, but was sanctioned by Athanasius—and Synesius though deprecating the degradation of the spiritual office confesses that in such cases " ἀνάγκη τὴν ἀκριβείαν παραβαίνεσθαι."—Ep. 67, p. 209, C.D.

Evagrius tells us that he was not baptized.* This seems incredible. An unbaptized person was obviously debarred from holding the lowest office in the Church, and Synesius, as we have already remarked,† would certainly not have omitted so important an objection in his letter to Evoptius. The same writer adds some remarks on his imperfect acquiescence in the doctrines of Christianity; but this is best brought out by an abstract of the letter addressed by him to his brother, which, as intended for the perusal of Theophilus and his friends in general, is worded in the most explicit language.

Ep. 105,
Abstract.

Synesius expresses his gratitude to the people of Ptolemais because they deem him worthy of so high an honour. He fears however lest he win man's favour at the cost of sinning against God.

His anxiety gives him no peace: his nights are sleepless. The burden of philosophy which he has borne so far was comparatively a light responsibility. But his success in that sphere has led men to over-estimate his character, and if he submits to the new charge he will run a risk of losing his reputation in two ways, by falling away from the old and failing to attain to the worthiness of the new. There are three main disqualifications: (i.) his religion was silent and solitary, an unparticipated joy. (ii.) His love of sport. Whenever he rises from his books, he is always ready for recreation of any kind. (iii.) His aversion by nature and habit to Political cares and business generally.

A bishop on the contrary should be: (i.) not a solitary worshipper, but one whose religion is visible to the eyes of his people; he must be a teacher of the law, and his doctrine must accord with it. (ii.) He must be averse to

---

* Evagrius (quoted in Migne. Patrol. Graeco-Lat., p. 104, 1, 2, Introd. to Synesius). I. 15.

† p. 49.

amusement (ἀμείλικτος). (iii.) He must be ready to take
part in any practical business that concerns the Church—he
must do the work of many men.

The last of the bishop's duties is the great stumbling-
block to Synesius. He finds the world too strong for the
spirit—he cannot serve two masters, as he puts it—and the
city life with its earth-ward tending cares will soon stifle the
divine spark within him. Moreover, he is not fitted by his
past life, which has not been free from faults and stains.
His conscience will weigh him down, and his philosophic
agnosticism will make him unable to dogmatise, and to give
answers explicit and positive as a priest should. He refuses
to give up his wife : "God and the law and the sacred hand
"of Theophilus gave her to me ; I declare therefore and
"bear witness to all men that I will not be separated from
"her, nor associate with her by stealth, like an adulterer.
"Paul and Dionysius, the elders who are chosen by the
"people, will tell Theophilus my resolution in this matter.
"It is a crucial point, and I regard other difficulties as
"trifling in comparison with it."

Synesius next touches on the difficulty of uprooting old
beliefs, especially the doctrines which philosophy has im-
pressed upon his reason. His old views are directly
opposed in fact to the popular views on more points than
one. (i.) He holds the pre-existence of the soul, as against
its creation subsequent to the body. (ii.) The world can
never be destroyed. (iii.) He regards the doctrine of the
resurrection as a sacred and ineffable mystery, but he is far
from agreeing with the popular notions on this subject.
(iv.) He considers that Reason permits a legitimate use of
lying in cases where the truth would only mislead.

If then he can be bishop on these terms—philosophizing
at home, talking in myths to the people—he might accept
the post. But if the priest has to be precise and dogmatic,

Synesius will have no disguises. he does not mean to preach doctrines in which he cannot believe. "What have "philosophy," he asks, "and the people in common?" The divine truth must be unspeakable; and as for dogmatism, the philosopher neither convicts nor is convicted—but his tongue will not contradict the feeling of his heart.

It will be a wrench in other ways. He cannot bear the thought of seeing his dogs idle, and his bow worm-eaten. Still he will endure whatever God commands; and if, after all he has said, Theophilus appoints him, then he accepts office as a Divine charge. For had the Emperor ordered it, he would have obeyed or met the penalty : to God surely a willing obedience is due.

The theological aspect of Synesius' reservations will be discussed elsewhere; but it is worth while to lay stress upon the conditions under which he submits to his election inasmuch as Druon has thought fit to dispute at some length the assumption that he "kept his wife and his "opinions."*

Did he keep his wife and his opinions. Anyone who reads the well-weighed words of Synesius himself cannot fail to be convinced that Druon is mistaken here. There was no compulsion brought to bear upon him;† he took his own line from the first and boldly stated his own terms. It is incredible that he should have drawn back and relinquished the advantages his frankness deserved. Besides, on the question of retaining his wife, there need have been no insurmountable difficulty—the Eastern

---

* Druon Études sur la vie et les œuvres de Synése.—pp. 42-43.

† See, however, Tillemont. Vol. xii., p. 519.—Il y a quelque apparence qu'on avait déja obtenu un ordre de l'Empereur (Theod. II.) et du Gouverneur de l'Égypte pour l'y contraindre. Et ceux qui estoient comme lui du corps de ville, n'en pouvaient être tirez que par un ordre de l'Empereur. But the passage at the close of Ep. 105 is surely metaphorical, only a supposition of what might have happened. λογίζομαι γὰρ ὅτι βασιλεως ἂν ἐπιτάξαντος . . . δίκην ἂν ἔδωκα μὴ πειθόμενος.

Church was always more liberal in this respect, and though towards the end of the fourth century the principle of celibacy was becoming general, rigid enactments on the subject were mainly confined to the west, and the evidence of Socrates who wrote about 439 A.D. declares the enforced celibacy of the higher clergy to be contrary to the custom of the Eastern Church.*

He says (Bk. v., c. 22, p. 241) that in the East though theoretically abstinence was usual, there was no legal compulsion in the matter—and he adds, "many Bishops "during their period of office have had children born to "them in lawful wedlock."

On the other hand, how are we to explain the conduct of Theophilus, which was so strange a contrast to his treatment of Chrysostom and the Origenists? How came he to consecrate as bishop a man who was certainly as much an Origenist as the Long Brothers, and whose appointment would be likely to raise a storm among the Anthropomorphic party?† To expect that God would work complete conversion in Synesius' heart after his consecration, was a possible idea for the clergy and people of Ptolemais, but not for the worldly Theophilus; and even if it were so, what *right* had he to baptise, much less make a bishop of a man whose faith was more than wavering? There are four possible reasons :—(i.) The urgent request of the whole

The conduct of Theophilus—theories accounting for.

---

* Vide Kraus, Tüb. Quart., vol. 47, p. 561.

Clausen and Hefele (Tüb. Quart., 1852, p. 147), both bear out this view. Was den Punkt seiner Ehe anlangt, so ist zu bedenken, dass er der Griechischen Kirche angehörte, und dass in dieser die Priester die vor ihrer Weihe eingegangene Ehe fortsetzen dürfen.

Cf. Can. 10. Synod of Ancyra, A.D. 314. Mansi, ii., p. 518.—It allows deacons to stipulate for a wedded life at the time of ordination; but after ordination, celibacy must be observed unless a condition to the contrary has been made.

† That Theophilus was fully acquainted with Synesius' views is evident from Ep. 105, 250 B, and 249 A.

body of the Church at Ptolemais: Theophilus would gain popularity by consenting. (ii.) Possibly an order from the Court.* (iii.) Synesius was personally acceptable to Theophilus, and not likely to thwart his ambition. (iv.) His ability and the good work he was likely to do as a bishop would reflect credit on Theophilus.

But there is a fifth reason adduced by Kraus (*Tüb. Quart.*, Vol. 47, p. 559) which is plausible and quite in keeping with what we know of Theophilus. It has already been noted what a field was offered by the Church for the ambition of Patrician families; and this was especially the case in the provinces where the power of the Church was not overawed by the proximity of the Court. Theophilus was notoriously ambitious and unscrupulous. He probably secured the primacy for his nephew, Cyril, after him, and would have liked to make the office a family appointment. To this end he was bound to be on good terms with the Court, and from this point of view it was clearly to his interest to win over a man of such birth and position as Synesius, with his wide circle of influential friends at Alexandria, and at Constantinople. This is why Theophilus first gave him a wife—probably from some friendly or allied family—and secondly appointed him without scruple bishop of Ptolemais. It does not seem beyond the bounds of probability that he caused rumours of Synesius' subsequent and full acceptance of Christian doctrine to be spread in Alexandria, with a view to checking the indignation of the orthodox; nor is it unlikely that these rumours may have given rise to the narratives of Evagrius and Photius.

Synesius' reluctance.

Synesius struggled hard to escape the office, but the entreaties of his people were irresistible: even the priests

---

* Tillemont, p. 519, referred to in note †, page 60.

pressed him to comply. And he overheard some old men, he tells us,* trying to remove his scruples by urging that "the demons had striven with God for him, and that by em-"bracing the better cause he would vex them; nay, even "though they assailed him, a philosopher consecrated to "God had nothing to fear."

In the same letter he describes the mental struggle, the doubts and difficulties with which he had to strive so sorely that he even prayed for death rather than to be bishop, and thought at times of quitting his country for ever, to escape so heavy a responsibility.† Theophilus allowed him seven months to consider the question. This was against rules, it is true, but the whole election was abnormal, and an extension of time is trivial beside the fact that Synesius was raised at a bound to high office in the Church without having served in any of the subordinate functions.

At last he yielded, not to human influence, as he reverently confesses, but to a feeling that it was the will of God, with whom all things are possible. Even after his consecration, however, he shrank for a time from entering upon his duties, and writes to the clergy of his diocese, begging them to offer prayers for him and for his people, and concluding with the words: "If God does not desert me, "I shall believe that my sacred office involved no fall from "philosophy, but an ascent to higher truth."‡ In another letter he urges his unfitness for the charge, and pleads to

---

* Ep. 57.

† Ep. 95. It is worth noting that this melancholy letter is written at the end of the seven months' deliberation—ὡς ἕβδομον ἤδη μῆνα γενόμενος ἐν τῷ δεινῷ.

‡ Ep. 11. Clausen ap Kraus. p. 550, suggests: Eine innere Stimme mochte ihm diese Annahme als eine Pflicht auferlegen für den Fall, dass der Κύριος τῆς χειροτονίας das Votum des Volks bestätigte.

ignorance of the scriptures.* But once Synesius had set his hand to the plough there was no turning back, and it is difficult to know whether to admire more the unselfishness with which he gave up all that was most dear to him, or the patience and determination with which, in spite of regrets, he entered on the difficult task which lay before him. There was soon need for the exercise of all these qualities.

Andronicus, the Governor of Pentapolis. Just about the time when Synesius became Bishop of Ptolemais, Gennadius the Syrian had laid down his office as Governor of Pentapolis, in which post he had acquitted himself honourably, and was succeeded by Andronicus the son of a poor fisherman of Berenice, one of the five towns in the province he was to rule. His appointment was wholly illegal, inasmuch as no native was eligible for the office of Governor in his own province.† but the corrupt court at Constantinople was amenable to bribes, and Andronicus attained his position by intrigue and systematic bribery.‡ He lost no time in showing his true colours.

It seemed as if the evil days of the republic had come back for the hapless provinces—with this difference, that Verres even, in this later age, would have found himself surpassed in cold-blooded cruelty.

---

* Ep. 13. This letter was sent with the paschal charge of Theophilus to his bishops, and Synesius urges Peter the Presbyter, who seems to have been in charge till his arrival, to pay special attention to the messenger who has braved the dangers of the journey, and passed through the midst of hostile tribes with his annual message.

† Gibbon. Vol. ii.. c. 17, p. 31. Ep. 73, 221 B.—Synesius paints in vigorous language the evils of a native Governor. "Send out to us," he says to Troilus, "men legally qualified to be our rulers, who know no one and are known of "none; who judge by common sense and not from individual whims. At "present the state of affairs is this : a man who was originally a thorn in the side "of the state sails back to be its tyrant, and carries on his political feuds from "the judgment seat. I say nothing of all the other evils that spring up in the "train of this one. A banquet is fruitful in false charges; and to gratify a "woman's caprice citizens are ruined."

‡ Ep. 58. τὴν ἀρχὴν . . . ὠνησάμενον.

It would be tedious to describe at length the outrages of this monster who showed an ingenuity in devising instruments of torture* that was worthy of a better cause. His agents were as ruthless as himself. Zenas, Julius, and above all Thoas, are mentioned as especial objects of detestation: they wrung fresh taxes from the impoverished people and executed with a refinement of cruelty the brutal orders of their master.

An instance will suffice:—Thoas had lately returned from Constantinople with the news of the illness of Anthemius, the Guardian of Theodosius II. He shamelessly alleged that Anthemius had been warned in a dream, that his recovery could only be ensured by the death of Maximinus and Clinias, two prominent citizens of Ptolemais who had unluckily incurred the hatred of the governor. They were actually arrested, beaten within an inch of their lives, and only spared by those demons for fresh tortures.†

The city was like a town taken by assault and given over to plunder. On every side, Synesius says, was wailing and lamentation.‡ All the plagues of past years seemed as nothing to this—locusts, earthquakes, barbarian inroads, famine, all had done their worst to the unhappy country, but their worst was light compared to the frightful oppressions and cruelties of this inhuman governor.‖ The laws were powerless—there was no one to enforce them— and the helpless citizens looked to their new bishop as a last resource.§ They were not disappointed.

* Ep. 79, and Ep. 58.

† Ep. 79., 226., D.

‡ Ep. 57.

‖ Ep. 73. Synesius alludes to an oracle ὅτι φθερεῖ τὰ Λιβύων ἡγεμόνων κακότης.

§ Ep. 57. δρόμος ἁπάντων εὐθὺς ἐπ' ἐμέ.

E

Synesius was not a man of strife, he was passionately
fond of peace and retirement, and yet some strange irony of
fate seemed ever to plunge him into the midst of unsought
conflicts. He had done Andronicus service at Alexandria
—had saved him in fact from imprisonment on two
occasions.* Gratitude for this might have been expected
from any other man, and the remonstrances of Synesius
should have come with double weight from a benefactor,
but Andronicus treated them with scorn. His insolence
was directed even against the Church : he violated the right
of sanctuary, and nailed his edict, threatening the most
cruel punishments to any priest who should harbour
fugitives, on the very doors of the sacred building.†

A citizen of some position was about to marry,
Andronicus forbade him, ordered his arrest, and had him
tortured in the mid-day heat, under a burning sun.
Synesius hurried to the spot, and, finding protest unavailing,
could only try to console the wretched victim by his
sympathy and presence. Andronicus in the meanwhile
gave vent to the most terrible blasphemies. " In vain," he
cried, " does he base his hopes on the church. My enemies
" shall not escape me, though they cling to the very feet of
" Christ himself."

Synesius' heart must have bled for his people. He had,
moreover, sorrows of his own to contend with ; one of his
sons had just died, and the burden of such accumulated
calamities must have been well-nigh intolerable. The
thought of ending his troubles by death seems even to
have crossed his mind.‡ The last resource of prayer failed
him,‖ and he was overcome with a sense of his own power-

* Ep. 79, 226 D.
† Ep. 58, 201-2.
‡ Epp. 57 and 79, 226 D.
‖ Epp. 57, 196, 197. νῦν πρῶτον οἶδα μάτην εὐξάμενος.

lessness. But there was a limit to forbearance : the measure was full to the brim. A letter to Troilus, whose influence with Anthemius was great, ended in no practical result.* Anthemius was probably too much exercised about the movements of Alaric to interfere; and as Alexandria seems to have been in imminent danger from the barbarians soon after these events, little help was to be expected from that quarter.† Prompt, drastic action was imperative, and Synesius roused himself for a great effort.

He convened a synod of the clergy,‡ probably from the whole district of the Pentapolis and there formulated the solemn sentence of excommunication which was to be launched against Andronicus, Thoas and their followers, if they still persisted in their course of outrage. The speech, for the 57th letter was nothing else, in which he makes a solemn indictment of Andronicus, and enters into a full account of his personal feelings, was probably delivered before the assembled people. He cannot perform the duties of a bishop as his people wish, the distraction of temporal cares is too much for him ; he calls on them to relieve him by appointing a successor, or at least a colleague in his responsibility.‖ They cried out against the proposal, and he caused the sentence of excommunication to be read. It was to be sent as a circular letter to the Christian churches throughout the world. ^{The Synod of Ptolemais.}

"The church of Ptolemais, to all the sister churches "throughout the world, addresses the following warning. "Let no temple be open to Andronicus and his followers, to "Thoas and his followers. Let every house of worship, ^{The sentence of excommunication.}

* Ep. 73.

† Tillemont, Vol. 12, p. 551. Catastasis, p. 300 B.

‡ Mansi. Concilia., iv., p. 2, leaves it a question whether this was a synod of bishops or presbyters.

‖ Ep. 57, 200.

"every sacred precinct, be closed to them. The Devil has
"no part in Paradise; if he enters by stealth he is expelled.
"Wherefore to all citizens and to magistrates I make this
"proclamation, that they go not under the same roof, or sit
"at the same table with these men. And above all to priests
"that they salute them not in their life-time nor grant them
"in death the rites of burial. But should anyone despise our
"church, for that our city is of small account, and shall
"receive these men whom it has excommunicated, thinking
"that they need not obey her because she is poor, then, let
"him know that he is dividing the church which Christ
"willed should be one; and whatever he be, Levite or
"presbyter or bishop, he shall be held by us as in the case of
"Andronicus, and we will refuse him the hand of greeting,
"nor eat at the same table with him. Finally we shall do
"anything rather than grant a share in the sacred mysteries
"to those who choose the part of Andronicus and of Thoas."*

Fall of Andronicus. Andronicus was thoroughly frightened at the thunders of the Church: he was down on his knees at once, promising repentance, and imploring forgiveness. But Synesius wisely mistrusted too prompt a submission, and, against the advice of his clergy, wished to enforce the decree by publishing it throughout the Churches. It was hard, however, for a new bishop, especially in Synesius' position, to run counter to the opinion of men who had grown old in the service of Christ; and sorely against his will he granted a delay to the offender, which was to last as long as he remained really penitent.† The consequence was what might have been expected. Before long Andronicus added fresh crimes to his charge and murdered a citizen under the most aggravated circumstances.‡ The

* Ep. 58. 203, A-B.
† Ep. 72, 218 C-D.
‡ Ep. 72, 219 C.

circular letter was promptly despatched to the various dioceses, and Andronicus met the ruin he deserved.

Even now the generous nobility of Synesius' character shone out brighter than ever. He shielded the wretched man from his enemies, and even pleaded his cause with Theophilus. The last words of his appeal are to the effect that if Theophilus protected him, it would be a proof to the wretched Andronicus that God had not entirely deserted him.* Perhaps he remembered the great scene in the Cathedral at Constantinople, when Chrysostom asserted the rights of sanctuary for the infamous Eutropius, and saved his life, for a time at any rate, from the fury of his enemies.

There is something very striking in this illustration of the power of the Church outside the spiritual sphere. It shews clearly what a security against tyranny and oppression a strong bishop might become, and proves even at this period the terrors of excommunication. The bishop was in fact a magistrate more than a preacher in these days. His office was a necessity of the troubled times in which men lived, and a safeguard of society. In fact, the line between civil and spiritual authority was not yet drawn, and though Synesius expresses his dislike of interference in the affairs of the world, we must remember that he is speaking from the point of view of a philosopher rather than that of a churchman,† and that his conduct towards Andronicus as it met the approval, so establishes the custom of the Church in that age.‡

Such was the episode of Andronicus—the most important event in the brief church life of Synesius. But it shows us only one, and that the sterner side of his character. He was by nature gentle and indulgent, yet without being

marginal note: The power of the Church illustrated by this event.

* Ep. 89, 230.
† Ep. 57.
‡ Cf. Note * on page 57.

weakly complaisant. His humility is evidenced by the deference he habitually showed toward his suffragan bishops: * his faithfulness and devotion to his friends, by the numerous letters addressed to them. But especially to be noted are the letters to Theophilus, which breathe the truest loyalty to his superior, maintaining at the same time an independent frankness which does honour to their intimacy.† It is in one of these that he puts before Theophilus the case of Alexander,‡ a native of Cyrene, who while still a youth had adopted the monastic life and filled the offices of deacon and priest in the church. Circumstances having brought him to Constantinople, he met Chrysostom there, and received at his hands consecration as Bishop of Basinopolis in Bithynia. This was before the great quarrel in the Eastern Church which ended in the exile of Chrysostom and the persecution of his followers. Alexander however remained faithful and without setting out to his see in Bithynia remained in Cyrene. Synesius' difficulty is how to treat him. Three years had passed since the amnesty by which the nominees of Chrysostom were released from disabilities, still Alexander lingered in his native town. The orthodox elders avoid him, and Synesius, though personally his friend, ignores him officially and does not admit him to the rights of a churchman. Is he a bishop or not? Theophilus' answer has not been preserved, but Synesius' allusion to Chrysostom in the letter is much to his credit, and makes us think better of the man to whom he is writing.

In this same case of Alexander was involved the wider question of the "vacantivi," roving church dignitaries who wished to have the honours of office without the burdens,

Synesius' relations as bishop to Theophilus.

The case of Alexander.

* Ep. 66.
† Ep. 66 and 67, and 9.
‡ Ep. 66.

and hung about any diocese wherever they saw a prospect of advantage. The council of Antioch in 341, ordained in its 17th canon that such men should be deprived even of communion, to compel them to return to their own churches.*

It is unfortunate, that with the exception of the homilies and a few short hymns, we have practically no serious theological work from Synesius' hand. The cares of the church, the troubles of his country weighed too heavily upon him. But we know that he did take some interest in the controversies of the age and that the heretics of his diocese were mistaken if they expected from him the indifference of a philosopher.

Treatment o Heretics— The Euno- mians.

There are still extant three letters written to him from Isidore, of Pelusium,† who, strangely enough, was one of the many victims of the jealousy and intrigues of Theophilus. They show that Synesius had applied to him for information on the doctrines of Nicaea ; and the instruction of Isidore, coupled with the advice to arm against the enemies of God, resulted in a crusade against the Eunomians‡—a sect who were trying to proselytize in the Pentapolis, and against whom, as children of the devil, he charges his clergy in no measured terms. They are to be persecuted, that is driven from the diocese, but without injury to property or person ; and the moderate nature of the measures proves conclusively that Synesius was simply acting with a view to Church discipline.

---

* Tillemont. Vol. xii., p. 540.

† Isidore, Letters, Bk. I., Epp. 232 and 318 ; Ep. 241 especially. ὃ βούλει μαθεῖν σύντομόν ἐστιν, ἀλλ' ὅμως ἀσφαλές· ἡ ἀεὶ ὡσαύτως ἔχει Θεὸς, ἡ μηδὲν προσκτᾶται πότε, ἀεὶ ἐστι καὶ πατήρ· ἡ δὲ ἀεὶ ἐστι πατήρ, ἀεὶ ἔσχε τὸν υἱόν· συναΐδιος ἄρα ὁ υἱὸς τῷ πατρί.

‡ Socrates. IV., 7. Eunomius, from whom the sect derived its name, was bishop of Cyzicus—he held the Arian heresy, and one of his doctrines was that " God knows no more than we do of his own existence."

But Synesius had other cares to distract him. Hardly was the country freed from the scourge of Adronicus when, towards the end of the same year, 410, the barbarians reappeared in more formidable force than usual. He had just lost one of his sons, and in the midst of his grief received a request from Theophilus to adjust an affair in his diocese that called for his personal attention and presence. Synesius, as metropolitan bishop, was to re-establish a see at Palaebisca, a small town which had once had a bishop* of its own, but had latterly fallen, with the approval of Theophilus, under the authority of the Church at Erythra, where the popular bishop, Paul, had won the hearts of all his flock. Synesius convened the citizens, and informed them of the will of Theophilus; but with one consent they implored him not to compel them to give up their beloved Paul. It was in vain that Synesius tried to assert his authority: his voice was drowned with the cries and tears of the crowd. The assembly was adjourned, but only to result in a repetition of the same scene. Synesius in the end was obliged to yield to their prayers, and he writes to Theophilus on the failure of his mission.† As there is no further allusion to the matter in his letters, we may assume that the people had their way.

The See of Palaebisca.

The dispute between Paul and Dioscorus. Synesius was at a loss to understand the secret of Paul's influence over the people. The dispute, however, in which he was involved a few days after must have opened Synesius' eyes as to his real character. An ancient fort stood on the confines of the dioceses of Erythra and Dardanis.‡ Dioscorus, the bishop of the latter diocese, was in possession, Paul demanded it of him, and upon his

---

* Vide note on p. 57. Migne, Vol. 78.

† Ep. 67.

‡ In those troubled times, a strong position of any kind was invaluable. παντὸς ἄξιον τοῖς κεκτημένοις.

refusal secretly established an altar in the building, and consecrated it as a place of worship. The other bishop, while disapproving of Paul's conduct, shrank from the idea of profanation in securing the rights of Dioscorus. But Synesius had no such scruples. His language is singularly firm and enlightened: "It has always been my wish to "distinguish between superstition and piety: superstition "is a vice that shields itself under the mask of virtue, nor "can philosophy see in it anything but a form of irreligion. "In my eyes there is nothing holy and sacred but what is "lawful and just. I have no fears about this so-called "consecration. No, true Christianity does not admit that "ceremonies and chants have the power in themselves to "draw down the Divine presence. God only descends into "souls free from passion and wholly submissive to His will. "How then can the Holy Spirit enter into a heart in which "anger and blind obstinacy are the motives of action, when "such passions banish it from the soul where it already "dwells?"*

The dispute, however, ended amicably. Paul bought the building from his rival, and both vied with one another in generosity.

To the same occasion belongs another incident which shows us Synesius in a sterner mood. Two priests, Jason and Lamponian, had come to blows, and caused great scandal.† The latter confessed his fault with tears, and his people begged that he might be forgiven. But Synesius was inexorable; he prohibited him from communion, and referred his case to Theophilus in whose hands he wished remission of the penalty to rest. Only, in case Lamponian should be on the point to die, any priest might administer the sacrament to him without hesitation. After giving a

* Ep 67, pp. 212, 213.
† Ep. 67, 215 A.

full account of these matters to Theophilus, Synesius enters
a complaint against the clergy of his diocese for mutual
accusation with a view to the favour of the civil powers.
He speaks of his own attempt to bring them by reproof
and censure to a better mind ; but he begs Theophilus to
strengthen his hands by a letter in the nature of a charge,
condemning such conduct in general terms and thus
enabling him to take active measures against the offenders.
He finishes this long letter, by asking the prayers of
Theophilus and lamenting the difficulties of his new
position.*

The
commander
Anysius.

Synesius returned to Ptolemais, and found the barbarians still encroaching. Fortunately a young commander,
Anysius, had been sent out at the close of 410,† and by his
courage and skill the danger was warded off for a time.
Anysius kept his troops well in hand by strict discipline, and,
dispensing with the Thracians and Marcommani, retained
only a chosen band of forty Unnigards whose courage he
had proved.‡ With this small force he worked wonders,
and his success is almost incredible. If he had only had
two hundred men like these, Synesius says, he might have
carried the war into the enemy's country and conquered
them decisively.‖

Synesius delivered a public eulogy on his services and
resolved to send a deputation to the Emperor begging that
Anysius might be left to them, and asking for a reinforce-
ment of 160 Unnigards. But Anysius was recalled, and
though the petition was urged and Anysius commissioned

His recall.

to plead with the Emperor himself (Anthemius, in other

* Ep. 67.
† Ep. 57. 193 B.
‡ Ep. 78. 223 C. οὗτοι δὲ δίς ἤδη καὶ τρὶς πρὸς ἄνδρας ὑπὲρ χιλίους τὸν
ἀριθμὸν μόνοι τετταράκοντα, μετὰ τὸν Θεὸν καὶ τὸν στρατηγοῦ παρετάξαντο.
‖ Elog. Anysii, 304 D.

words)—it fell through; and his successor Innocent, an old man and an invalid,* soon undid all the advantages Anysius had gained.

The last glimpse of hope seemed to have died away for the unhappy country, and the clouds closed in on every side. The Ausurians returned with fresh forces: the whole country was devastated, the people reduced to slavery, the churches desecrated or burned. Ptolemais was besieged— Siege of Ptolemais. at one time Egypt itself seemed in danger.†

In the hour of his country's distress, Synesius was once more overwhelmed with a domestic calamity.‡ His second Death of his second son— son died, and he writes a despairing letter on the ruin of all the Catastasis. his hopes. To this period belongs the *Catastasis*, a speech in which he deplores the disasters of the province, and gives vent to such gloomy forebodings that Tillemont‖ is justified in supposing that it was never delivered. It is one long wail from beginning to end; and there is something unmanly about his despair which even suggests to him the thought of flight to some distant island, where he will dwell a stranger and a wanderer, far from the reach of the Ausurians. Such language could only have dispirited the people whom it was his duty to exhort and strengthen; and Tillemont's theory is not only the most charitable, but also the most rational, when we see that Synesius' acts were nobler than his words, and that he was still as ready as ever to do his duty. So far, in fact, from confining himself to idle complaints, he was simply indefatigable throughout the siege, taking his stand on the battlements and watching through the night: inspiring everywhere, by his presence

* Catastasis. 307 A. τί γάρ ἂν τις αἰτιάσαιτο τὸν ἀναίτιον ᾧ κάι γῆρας βαθύ, κάι νόσου καταβολὴ πολυχρόνιος;

† Catast., p. 300 B.

‡ Ep. 88.

‖ Tillemont, XII., p. 551.

and example, the sinking courage of his countrymen.*

The town was saved for a time, and the Ausurians were driven back. Marcellinus conquered them more or less decisively in the following year, 413, and they withdrew, leaving, however, only ruins behind them, and a country hopelessly impoverished.† The Pentapolis never recovered to any extent from this last invasion, and the blessings of peace seemed to have come too late for the unhappy

The last of his children dies. people. To Synesius, at any rate, the relief was outweighed by a fresh disaster‡—the last of his children died.

There is something very pathetic in the closing year of

Synesius falls ill. his life. He was worn out by anxiety and distress. All that he loved best was taken from him. The very people he had served so well, were well nigh as down cast as himself. By a strange coincidence, what seems to be his last letter was addressed to Hypatia. It was written on the sick bed from which, in all probability, he never rose.‖

Letter to Hypatia. "I have dictated this letter lying on my couch. May it "find you well, my mother, sister, teacher; you who in all "these relations have done good to me......My physical "weakness springs from mental prostration. The recollec- "tion of my lost children is wearing me slowly away. "Synesius should have lived only so long as he could "escape the evils of life......Would that I might either cease "to live, or else forget the tombs of my children."

Plan of founding a monastery. One other letter written at this sad time is of peculiar interest.§ From it we learn that Synesius intended to found a monastery, an ἀσκητήριον, and it is not unlikely that in his troubles, half wearied as he was of life, he wished for

* Catast., p. 302, B.C.
† Ep. 62.
‡ Ep. 70.
‖ Ep. 16. Cf. Ep. 80.
§ Ep. 126.

complete retirement and contemplated spending his declining days there.

There is not however the shadow of a tradition that would justify the theory that he did so retire. After the year 413 there is a blank in his history, and the absence of letters or writings of any sort after that date points to his death about this time.

In 413 then, or 414, Synesius passed away—to join his children as he had prayed to do. Still in the prime of life, with a great career possibly of usefulness before him, he might have left us writings whose fame would have enrolled him among the greater Fathers of the Church. *Dis aliter visum.*

We can only count him happy in that he did not live to see his friend and teacher torn to pieces by a mob of fanatics in the name of the religion in whose service he had died.*

Synesius dies, 413-14.

---

* Hypatia was murdered in 415. It is incredible that if Synesius had survived this date he should have left no mention of her awful fate in his writings.

A LEGEND OF SYNESIUS.—Two centuries later, Moschus, in a work entitled *The Spiritual Meadow*, narrates the following legend of Synesius, which Tillemont somewhat naïvely refers to as "l'un des plus riches ornemens de la tradition de l'Église sur le sujet de l'aumosne." It may not unfitly find a place at the end of Synesius' life, as the sole traditionary record of a later age. A pagan philosopher, Evagrius, who (like Synesius himself) refused to believe in the end of the world, or a corporeal resurrection, was at length converted by our bishop. He was still, however, troubled by grave doubts as to the future state and the recompense which Christ had promised—an hundred-fold to all who shewed mercy to the poor in this life At last he put into Synesius' hands 300 pieces of gold for the poor, exacting from him a written promise that Christ would reward him in the world to come. Soon after, the philosopher died, and on his death-bed charged his children to bury him with the document clasped in his hands. Three days after the burial, he appeared to Synesius in a dream and bade him come and take from his hands the deed, for the debt had been paid in full. The tomb was opened, and the paper found in the dead man's hand, only with a written acknowledgment freshly added by Evagrius himself, acknowledging the receipt of his due, and relinquishing all claims against Synesius. This business-like document was preserved, adds the writer, among the treasures of the Church at (Cyrene?) Ptolemais.

THE

PHILOSOPHY OF SYNESIUS.

THE PHILOSOPHY OF SYNESIUS.

THE difficulty of dealing with Synesius as a philosopher appears at first sight less formidable than is really the case. As a matter of fact, his contribution to thought is small; only two of his writings are professedly philosophical, and their scope is narrow and their treatment popular. Add to these the scattered allusions in his letters and rhetorical works, the mystic rhapsodies of the Earlier Hymns, and we have mentioned all that is left of the philosophy of Synesius.

A system it is not, and it would be absurd to expect a system from a man who not only died, as far as we can tell, in the prime of life, but the best of whose years were spent in restless strife and wearing cares, and whose tastes leaned rather to the trifling pursuits of an amateur, than to the sterner studies of a true philosopher.

So far the task would seem a light one; but as all thought is the outgrowth of previous ages and needs their study for its apprehension; so Synesius is linked to the past and to his contemporaries on every side, and if we are to understand his views, we must first try, however inadequately, to realise theirs.

Zeller[*] has well expressed the key-note of the last Characteristics centuries of the ancient world. It was a time when the of the thought universal feeling of alienation from God and the yearning after a higher revelation came naturally upon men who had lost faith in the old creeds and had not yet found harmony with the new.

[*] Zeller. Die Philosophie der Griechen, III., 2, pp. 369, ff.

F

The Materialistic moral systems of Zeno and Epicurus had failed to satisfy the cravings even of the cultured few. A return to metaphysics was inevitable. Scepticism had done its work, and by suggesting that truth which could not be attained in the form of intellectual knowledge might be discovered by some other means, such as religious tradition or even direct revelation, prepared the way for Neo-Platonism.

It was an eclectic age. "Just as the Empire was a "congeries of nations artificially held together round the "will of an irresponsible prince, so Neo-Platonism united "all elements of existing philosophical schools into one "comprehensive system with a Being lying beyond it; "and soaring above every notion that experience and "conception can supply, causing all things, but subject to "no causality."*

The writings of Plato were regarded, so to speak, as the Bible of the Neo-Platonic school, a kind of revealed record ; and originality of thought was thus stifled at the outset by the growing tendency to dogmatism. The idea of truth as the goal of philosophy was being resigned for the truth to be found only in an emotional apprehension of the divine.

On the other hand there was fortunately a principle of growth in the diversity of nationality, and so of thought, which made Alexandria the Athens of its age. The East once more asserted its influence over the West and "as "Byzantine Imperialism combined Oriental despotism with "the Roman idea of the state, so Neo-Platonism filled out "with Oriental Mysticism the scientific forms of Greek "philosophy."†

The Oriental tendency may be traced most clearly in the conception of God as the transcendent rather than the

* Zeller.
† Ibid.

immanent cause of the world, and in the notion of asceticism as the essential form of morality. As contrasted with the philosophy of Plato there is a deeper difference still. The investigation of nature and of man was now secondary to the enquiry into the relations of man to God, and his possible union with Him.

Briefly to sum up the main doctrines common to the various schools of the age we may again quote from Zeller.

"The dualistic opposition of the divine and earthly. An "abstract conception of God, excluding all knowledge of "the divine nature. Contempt for the world of sense, on "the ground of the Platonic doctrine of matter and of the "descent of the soul into the body from a superior world. "The theory of intermediate potencies or beings through "whom God acts upon the world of phenomena. The need "of ascetic self-emancipation from the bondage of sense: "and faith in a higher revelation to man when in a state "called enthusiasm."

All these doctrines will be found in Synesius, and they will be best discussed by the help of illustration from his writings and comparison with the treatment of the same ideas by the writers to whose influence he owed so much.

To begin then with the more abstract notions, the metaphysics of his creed, as expounded, mainly in the earlier hymns. *Metaphysics of Synesius.*

The Supreme Being, the One of Plotinus, is transcendent and alone existent, if indeed existence can be predicated of what is ἐπεκεῖνα τῆς οὐσίας.* It is above and beyond Gods and mind ;† it cannot therefore be comprehended, much less defined.

It is true that in our endeavours to grasp the idea of God we give him names and ascribe qualities to him, but

---

* Plotinus, Enn. I., 7·1.
† H. III., 164.

they are wholly inadequate, and only serve as makeshifts relatively to ourselves.*

God is the unknowable, the unspeakable ;† and our wisest attitude towards such a mystery is the silence of humility.‡ At the most, we can only say what God is not, and Theology so far is negative. It may seem superfluous to add that " the Supreme " is without feeling|| and dwells girt with the mysterious awe of an eternal silence.§ Such is " the father and ruler of all things, unbegotten, who sits " on the heights of heaven, rejoicing in imperishable glory, " God immovable, the Blessed unity of unities, the first " monad of monads."

Such at least is the metaphysical notion of the Neo-Platonic Unity when logically applied : but in practise the theory led to inevitable contradictions. This supreme unity is the first cause of all things ; but it is a necessity of its nature that it should not energise. There must then be an intermediary, a secondary cause : which, however, derives its existence and its power from the One which alone is. The chasm between God and the world must be bridged over: yet the Neo-Platonists by their assumptions as to the Divine Essence made such union logically impossible. And so they peopled the space between God and the world with intermediate beings, metaphysical entities or demons.

It is thus we find Plotinus speaking of the One as ἀρχή, then as δύναμις, or even ἐνεργεία—and when Synesius, in his hymns, says that the Supreme Being is both one and many, one in itself and pervading all things,¶ he is clearly leaning

* *De Regno*, p. 8.
† H. IV., 227.
‡ H. I., 75.
|| *Dion.*, p. 45.
§ H. II., 23.
¶ H. III., 200. ἓν καθ' ἑαυτὸ καὶ διὰ πάντων. Cf. III., 190.

towards the more logical idea of Pantheism which was Plato's ultimate goal.

To return to the One. From the excess of its energy, Plotinus says it sends forth an ·image of itself,* just as the sun shoots out its rays. *The Plotinic Trinity.*

This image is "Mind," the Spirit of the Universe. It is also one, one in itself and one with the supreme unity from which it sprang. But while "Mind" is one it is not so pure a unit as τὸ Ἕν,† for it contains immanent within itself the Ideas, not however as mere thoughts but as integral parts of itself. They form the κόσμος νοητός, the true world of thought, of which this world is but the shadow.‡

Lastly, "Mind" in its turn produces as its image the soul,‖ which though inferior in rank and character is still divine. The soul begets the corporeal, and permeates the body it begets, the universe, as fire permeates air. In Synesius' own words, the Third God is the world-soul, the immediate creator of us men and the universe in which we live.§

But though soul is here recognised as the immediate creator of the universe, the creative act is to be referred through "Mind" to the absolute One; and thus Synesius' language is not really inconsistent with the language of Plotinus when he speaks of "Mind" as the δημιουργός working through soul,¶ and it would be easy to multiply passages from the Hymns, in which wisdom or mind is clearly recognised as the creator, and soul as the necessary

* H. I., 83, ἀπόρρωξ.
† H. III., 213. Cf. IV., 69.
‡ Ep. 44, 182.
‖ Plotinus Enn. 5, 1, 7.
§ Calv. Encom., p. 71.
¶ Plotinus Enn., 2. 3. 18.

medium of Mind, just as Matter is essential to the actualisation of soul.*

Kraus† is inclined to trace two stages in the early doctrine of Synesius on the Plotinic Trinity. In the first and second Hymns, the Supreme One sends forth a monad which in its turn acquires a triple force.‡ In the third and fourth, the first monad no longer sends out a second but is itself Father, Son, and Spirit.||

Esoteric vagueness and mystery. It is impossible, however, to collect any definite doctrine from the rhapsodical utterances of these earlier hymns. The language is too vague, the exposition too fragmentary. Moreover, it is clear that Synesius would probably have been as mystified himself if called on to explain his views. He stops short in the midst of some theological rapture and enjoins silence on the too audacious lyre.§ This philosophic reserve, this reluctance to reveal the secrets of Divine wisdom comes out prominently in many passages of his writings.

The *profanum vulgus* was a terrible bugbear to the Neo-Platonist, but in the fourth century A.D. there was sufficient freedom of philosophic thought at any rate to make precautions unnecessary, and the nervous apprehension lest some unspeakable truth should reach the ears of the common herd who certainly would not have understood its meaning, looks very like affectation and is a weak point

---

* H. II., 27.   III., 203.   κλεινὰν σοφίαν δημιόεργον.   III., 563-8.
IV., 164.   νοῦς, the creator.   νοῦς ψυχοδότας.

† Tüb. Quart., Vol. XLVII., p. 592.

‡ H., I., 63, 70.

|| H., IV., 123.   Cf. III., 212, and IV., 117.   μόνας ἢ τρίας ὢν, τρίας ἢ μόνας ὤν.

§ Hymn. I., 70.

in a system which does not err on the side of lucidity.*

This threefold division of the One, in its different aspects, which reminds us at once of the Christian doctrine of the Trinity is brought out more or less clearly in the Hymns.

The One in a passage already quoted† is referred to as

μονάδων μόνας πρώτη·
αὐτόσσυτος ἀρχά·
ὅθεν αὐτὴ προθόρουσα
διὰ πρωτόσπορον εἶδος
μόνας ἀῤῥήτα χυθεῖσα
τρικόρυμβον ἔσχεν δικάν.

It is true that Mind and Soul are not specifically mentioned, but the passage, in so far as it is comprehensible, must refer to the Plotinic Trinity. The following passage in the Second Hymn ‡ is more explicit and recalls in a striking manner the very titles of God in the Christian doctrine.

"For where the Paternal depth is, there also is the "glorious Son even Wisdom the creator of the world, and "there shines the reconciling light of the Holy Spirit."

One more passage deserves to be quoted as illustrating the successive grades in this strange theology. It occurs in the *De Providentia* ‖ and may be summarised briefly thus. There are three grades of Gods. First comes the πηγή or source of Being—it rests unmoved in the fulness of its own perfection. This is clearly the One.

---

* Tillemont, vol. xii., p. 502. The Neo-Platonists, "faisaient un mystère de "leur philosophie et observaient un grand secret pour ne pas communiquer "aisément à d'autres."

Synesius avoids discussing τὰ ἀπορρητά in his letters lest they should fall into the hands of the uninitiated, and he censures Herculian severely for our indiscretion in this matter. cf. Ep. 105, 136, 142, and *De Prov.* 128.

† H. I., 52-70.
‡ H. II., 27.
‖ *De Prov.*, 97-8.

Next we have, γένος θεῶν ὑπερκόσμιον.* This embraces all that *is* in the true sense of the word. (sc. the Ideas.) It is wholly independent and averse from Matter and its end is to contemplate the source (πήγη) from which it arises. Here we have the Mind (νοῦς) of Plotinus.

Lastly there are "ὁι φύσει Θεοί."† They are concerned with the sphere of what becomes and changes, and are the immediate agents of God in his dealings with the world. These must represent the ψυχή, the world-soul which Synesius speaks of as the Third God.

The three grades of deities just referred to, are indicative of the inherent weakness of Neo-Platonism as a religion. A God who is a mere philosophical abstraction could not and can never satisfy the spiritual cravings of men, and so the spiritual world had to be repeopled, and a system which started with unity as its principle ended in mere Polytheism and superstitions grosser still.

God gives birth by emanation to a crowd of inferior deities, who form a complete hierarchy between the extreme terms of the One and Matter. From the world-soul we pass by a descending scale to the evil demons or powers of darkness —beings who are neither spirit nor matter, but partake of the nature of both.‡ These are the powers that "day and "night for our destruction wait."‖

On the other hand, the old heroes, the demi gods of the Greek mythology, reappear as the guardians of men, their good demons. The heavens are peopled with angels (στράτος ἀγγέλων ἄγηρως) that watch over man in obedience to the Divine will.§

* H. III., 269.
† H. II., 40.   III., 279.
‡ Druon, p. 187.
‖ H. IV., 245.
§ H. IV.. 265.

Matter is τῶν ὄντων ἔσχατον—but it exists and is eternal, Matter—the existence of the Evil.
in so far as it is bound up in soul. For the separation of
Form and Matter is only logical, and there never was a time
when this universe was not, nor will it ever cease to be.[*]
This is a doctrine that Synesius insisted upon, before he
submitted himself for consecration. Matter is the body of
the soul (ὄχημα ψυχῆς), its emanation. Soul needed matter,
in which to externalize itself.[†] The soul therefore has a twofold aspect, a divine nature and one less pure.

For the first of existences are simple, but their nature,
by descending to union with the material, is diversified.[‡]
The κόσμος is not the absolute one, but the one composed of
many, it is a living *animal;* a mysterious harmony pervading the vast whole.

The explanation of the origin of evil by matter as an
ἀνάγκη, not a rival power but a necessary condition for the
externalization of thought, is the doctrine of Plato in the
Timæus. Evil, however, in his theory, is non-existent, all
existence is good, and what we think to be evil only seems
so to our imperfect apprehensions. The Neo-Platonists
look upon evil as more of a reality, and betray, though in a
very modified form, the Oriental Dualism which appears so
markedly in the Gnostic writers.

Synesius is not explicit on the question, but we may
conclude from the *De Providentia* that he regarded evil as
a necessity, a means in God's hand for the discipline of
mankind.[||] The evil spirits are his ministers and he directs
their machinations to ultimate good.[§] Misfortune is a
chastening influence, and the troubles of life are not in vain

---

* Ep. 105.
† Plot. Enn., IV., 3, 9.
‡ Calv. Encom.. p. 69, D. 71 c. *De Insomn.*, 132 D).
|| *De Prov.*, 98.
§ Ep., 57.

if they make us discontented with material things. For the soul would never shake itself free from the body unless it had to encounter evil in the affairs of this life.* What then is the relation of God to man? What is the Divine Economy in so far as it concerns us? This question leads naturally to the theory of Providence set forth in the work *De Providentia.*

.   .   .   .   .   .

Outline of the *De Providentia.*

An outline of the *De Providentia* has been already given,† and its historical position defined. The question of the Divine Economy is introduced as follows :—The friends of Osiris foreseeing the future, urge him to banish Typho, and predict the fatal consequences of a weak indulgence, not only to himself but to mankind. Osiris replies that if the gods continue propitious and help him he has no fear of Typho.‡ But his father interrupts him and points out the folly of such confidence. There are three grades of Gods. The highest is the source of all things, God Supreme ; the next is the race of Gods above the world, and neither of these can endure contact with matter in any form. This is left for the lowest grade of deities, to whom the immediate government of the world is therefore delegated.

As a counterpoise, however, to their influence, there are the powers of darkness : evil demons whose nature is wholly opposed to the divine calm of the Gods, and whose restless malice finds a congenial sphere in the world of matter.

Now matter, the basis of this world of sense, is in itself inert and incapable of self preservation. God, therefore, is obliged to turn his attention to it from time to time, and organizing its disorder he transmits a certain impulse in the right direction, which avails however only

* *De Insomn.,* 139.
† v. p. 30.
‡ *De Prov.,* 98.

until its force is spent. For matter has no originating
power in itself and can only obey the influence of the
Divine hand which alone contains the principle of motion.
Just as puppets moved by strings fall limp and helpless
when the hand is withdrawn, so the fortunes of the world
fluctuate, according as the influence of God is newly
given or on the wane. We owe all good things to the
Gods, and their action, as it concerns us, can only be bene-
ficial, but it is not exercised in unbroken continuity.

We must remember that it is no pleasure for the higher
powers to set the world to rights; nay rather, an unwelcome duty, for it involves a departure from their higher
nature, a turning from things divine to the baser concerns
of the material. (99) Contemplation is their highest function, the ordering of the world is secondary to it, and
only exercised under the pressure of necessity. And,
therefore, we must not expect the Gods to stand by us
always, remembering that they are far removed from us
in heaven and have a purer sphere wherein to energize.

Man must help himself, must strive to raise himself
heavenwards, instead of trying to bring the Gods down
to his own level. The struggle of matter with spirit is
often a sore one. The powers of evil who oppose man
are in their proper element; and we need the strength
of youth and the wisdom of age to overcome. (100) The
Gods look down on our endeavours and in due time,
when succour is needed, they will give it, but the appointed
times are not for us to know. We must rely on our own
strength while we can, for there is no greater impiety than
to misuse through faint-heartedness the means of defence
we possess, and then to call on the Gods for aid before the
proper crisis for their interference has arrived.

(111) Even when hope seems a mockery, we must
not despair. There is a lesson for us even in misfortune,

and God often withholds his aid until the most irrational of men have discerned their own helplessness and the difference between good and evil.

Remarks on the theory of Providence. Well might Synesius approve the saying that man is the plaything of God, if such is indeed the providence that guides our destinies. The God of his system is the philosopher idealised. Action degrades him, and is only submitted to under compulsion. And thus while the attitude of man in this strange theory recalls the Stoic resignation, the attitude of God suggests the indifference and selfish calm of the Deities of Epicurus.

It is a poor consolation to know that God will only interfere at fixed epochs, and when the Good in the world is on the verge of extinction. Providence of this spasmodic nature is as unsatisfying as it is unphilosophical. Possibly the troubled times in which Synesius lived inclined him to this view, which concedes so much to the enemies of light and goodness. As he witnessed Aurelian retiring into exile, and Gainas the savage Goth triumphant; as he foresaw the threatened extinction of the old civilization by barbarian hordes; he may have felt that his generation was passing through an age of trial, and that God had withdrawn awhile from the world.

Epilogue to the *De Providentia*. Synesius adds, by way of epilogue to the history of Osiris and Typho, two philosophic questions which are not of any great importance, but may as well receive a passing notice. The first might have suggested to him the Rule of Law as the clue to the mystery of the universe, rather than the fitful government of a misnamed Providence.

(127) Why is it that history repeats itself, so that old men witness with their own eyes what they read of as boys or heard from their grandfathers? His explanation is this: The universe is a whole, complete in itself, and all its parts are in mutual dependence and sympathise with one another.

The laws therefore which regulate the movements of the heavenly* bodies must affect the course of events on earth. Their influence makes itself felt in the destiny of men and nations, and when, with the lapse of time, the stars, after accomplishing their revolutions, return to their original positions before beginning their course anew, the progress of events starts with them from the old standpoint, and the past is thus ever being reproduced in the present.

One need not look far for the source of this doctrine, which corresponds closely to the Stoic theory of cycles, which in its turn may be traced back to the theories of Aristotle.†

The second question he raises is,—" How is it that good " and evil spring so nearly from the same source, so that the " most violent contrast is possible between the nearest " relations ? " The explanation is very singular. In all things, good and evil are blended. But if by the purifying agency of virtue a sharp line of distinction is drawn between the two, then gradually the good is sifted from the evil : and so while an elder son exhausts the evil propensities of his race, a younger than he may embody its perfections.

So far we have considered God in his relations to man. Man's relation The question remains :—What is man's relation to God ? to God. What is our nature and our destiny ?

The Idea of the world-soul of which our individual souls are parts, was a notion common to all the metaphysical schools.‡ With Plato, Synesius held that the soul is pre-

---

* The universe is to Synesius a sphere (H. IV., 154-60). The world-soul permeates it, and so each portion wills with the will of the whole, all being linked together by a common sympathy. Our world occupies the centre, around it lies the belt, first of air and then of ether. The stars are endued with life—they have souls and are themselves Gods. High above them is the circle of the fixed stars, and beyond that the ῥόος ἀστέρων ἔρημος, the abode of silence and eternal calm where God dwells.

† Metaphysics, A. c. VIII., 19-21.

‡ H. III., 588-590.

existent and has lived other lives before entering into its present body, and will pass through yet more stages of existence before it is merged again in the world-soul from which it was derived.* For the source and the destiny of the soul is one and the same : and the belief in individual immortality nowhere appears in the writings of Synesius.

Our life here is a long struggle. Evil is self-taught, virtue is to be acquired by toil alone, and the soul is always in imminent danger of falling under the yoke of matter. There is a passage in the third hymn which expresses at once the position of man and his aspirations.

" Grant to me that I may escape the plague of my body
" and pass at one swift bound to thy halls, to thy bosom,
" whence floweth forth the fountain of life. I, a drop of
" heavenly dew, am shed upon the earth. Restore me to
" the source from whence I was poured out a wandering
" exile. Grant me to be merged in the primal light. . . . .
" that I pass no more under the taint of earth."†

The Psychology of Synesius.

The fullest account, however, of Synesius' psychology is to be found in the work entitled *De Insomniis*,‡ and a brief summary of his view may well precede the discussion of the remarkable theory of Divination therein set forth.

Abstract of the *De Insomniis*.

(134) The mind contains the forms of things that really are (νοητὰ), the soul the images of those that become—and, as there is a link between mind and soul, namely reason, so Imagination (φαντασία) forms the link between the soul and the senses. (136) It is in fact the sense *par excellence*—sight, hearing, touch, are all auxiliary to it and radiate from it as a common centre. But while they act outwardly, it

* H. I., 100.
† H. III., 706. Cf. H. IV., 290 to end.
‡ This work was composed in a single night. v. Ep. 153, 293, A., a letter to Hypatia with a copy of the treatise.

receives their impressions within and presents them as in a mirror to the soul.

While thus to the senses Imagination is a ruling force, swaying the animal as from a citadel, it is wholly inferior to the soul, as the soul in turn is inferior to the mind ; and its position is midway between the rational and irrational, the bodily and the incorporeal.* In Synesius' own words it is ὄχημα θειοτέρας ψυχῆς. But though in a way disparaged as compared to the more divine element in man, φαντασία is necessary to the soul and is received by the soul on its descent from the celestial spheres, that it may have something in which to embody itself. (137) We cannot think without the aid of imagination, except when by some rare good fortune we attain the conception of immaterial form. But while we are in the world of matter, we are compelled to live and move through material agencies, and our everyday life is one of imagination, or at any rate of reason employing imagination as its servant.

What we can do however, and what we must do if we are to rise to higher things, is to keep our material faculties as pure and unsullied as we can. The soul must raise the imagination or fall with it.

(138) Vice loads the wings of the aspiring spirit, virtue lightens them by blotting out the stains of evil. This is what Heraclitus had in mind when he spoke of the dry soul that rises by very lightness heavenward, while the soiled damp spirit finds earth more akin.

(139) The joys of this world are the lures of the lower powers. The soul which at parting drinks a Lethaean draught, is offered at its entry upon life a cup of intoxicating sweetness.

---

* The different names given to φαντασία in the course of the treatise bring out its twofold nature.

It has a service to perform but it submits to a slavery,* and once within the clutches of matter, finds it hard to tear itself loose. Still though the soul may fall to terrible depths of degradation, it is possible by toil and successive stages of existence to purify and raise it.† And strangely enough, in its rising, it takes with it, quite naturally, according to Synesius, this *imagination* which it received as a trust from the celestial bodies.

(141) This semi-corporeal, semi-spiritual element, therefore, would seem to pervade a higher sphere than ours, and to attain a co-existence with the soul. For the soul after its ascent is the treasure-house of truth ; it is pure, clean and undefiled, foreseeing the future as a God.

Clearly then it is our duty in this life to purify and keep unsullied the *imagination* which is so closely bound up in the soul. (142) Philosophy alone can ensure this end and enable the soul to rise above the complexity of change to the unity of the spiritual. Man must therefore keep himself aloof as far as possible from the affairs of the world, leading the life of intelligence and only descending when compelled to the degradation of active interference.

While thus contemplation by purifying the soul elevates us to God, so by a kind of attraction it draws God nearer to us. But if we fail to develop τὸ θεῖον within us to its full extent (and the brain must be filled with πνεῦμα of one kind or the other) then nature, abhorring a vacuum, will step in and fill the void space in our brains with evil spirits. This is the punishment of those godless men who defile the divine element within them.

The whole theory is full of inconsistencies. At bottom it is simply another attempt to bridge over the gulf between spirit and matter. The soul *quâ* soul cannot take cogni-

* H. III. 571.
† H. I. 100. ἵνι καὶ δεῦρο πεσόντων ἀναγώγιός τις ἀλκά.

zance of matter, and so an intermediate faculty is introduced superior to sensation but inferior to soul. How far is this spiritual, how far material? Synesius allows to it a share in both natures, and at one time insists on the former, at another on the latter aspect of it.

The lower animals possess it: yet by its means we may rise to a higher region and it would seem that it shares in a measure the immortality of the soul. In brief the theory is a compromise between the spiritual and the material psychologies.

Soul, according to Plato, is a unity, unextended and immaterial, yet with Synesius the divine occupies a definite space in the brain of man. In Plato, though the soul has a rational and irrational aspect, its unity as a spirit is carefully preserved. The irrational functions of the soul exist only in conjunction with the body and cease when the relation comes to an end.

But Synesius prolongs the existence of φαντασία, allows it to rise with the soul from earth, and leaves us in doubt how far its corporeal nature extends.

The aim however of this psychological investigation is to establish the scientific value of divination by dreams. *The value of Divination by Dreams.*

The Stoics had rejected the notion of miraculous interposition, but held that if there is an unbroken chain of cause and effect, there must be signs indicative of causes from which effects that may be known result: and the soul of man must be able to observe under certain circumstances what generally escapes his notice. The regularity of nature, the modern argument against divine interposition, is, with Synesius, an argument in favour of it.

(132) The world is a complete whole, a living being, all of whose parts are linked in harmony, and act upon one another naturally. The wise man seeks to understand these mutual relations between things and the fixed laws by which

G

they act, and, as the result of this knowledge, he gains an insight into the future through the aid of divination.

Synesius touches lightly on the various modes of augury and then proceeds to discuss the utility of dreams in this matter. Here the imagination comes in. To obtain clear and true visions, the imagination must be purified, and this purity is essential to clear vision of the truth by day as well as by night, in our waking and in our sleeping dreams.

(143) The pursuit of divination thus becomes a training for the higher life (ἀναγώγη ψυχῆς.) A man must banish all evil thoughts and passions from his mind, and treat his bed as it were the Pythian tripod. He must be moderate in his appetites, and in a word avoid all that tends to weaken the spiritual element within him. Moreover, the simplicity of the method has many advantages, and here Synesius indulges in indirect depreciation of the popular systems of augury.

(144) There is no expensive ritual necessary. No elaborate apparatus is required. No distant journey to some sacred shrine. Rich and poor, the man of business, and the man of leisure, all can avail themselves of it, for it costs nothing and causes no waste of time, inasmuch as a man has only to take advantage of the sleep which nature demands. There is something impious about the ordinary divination ; it seems an attempt to wrest God's secret will from him. But in sleep we are merely the passive recipients of the divine message. The soul finding a lull from the tide of sense-impressions,* which distract it by day, presents its images (εἴδη) to reason, pure and undefiled, καὶ τὰ πρὸς τοῦ Θεοῦ πορθμεύει.

(148) Synesius adds his own experience. He finds that half-finished problems were worked out in sleep ;

---

* Cf. H., VI., 27. τερσάινων ὀλόους κλύδωνας ὕλας.

and especially in matters of style dreams brought him many a valuable lesson. Then again he devised snares for the beasts of chase in his sleeping hours. But most of all, this divination stood him in good stead at Constantinople where he was warned in a dream against the delusions of magic, and inspired with confidence when brought into the Imperial Presence.

But a new difficulty arises. So far only dreams whose message is clear and unmistakeable have been spoken of; there remains a far larger class of the mysterious kind. Here art and science come into play, although no special rules can be laid down, and treatises which attempt to do so only stultify their authors. A few general principles may be stated.

Each man should keep a record of his dreams and note what events or circumstance preceded or followed after; so that just as the pilot recognises a headland and knows by experience that a certain city lies behind it, so by dreams we should know that certain events follow on certain presages.

So far the treatise is philosophical in a way, and there is a certain beauty in the idea of God visiting man in sleep and conversing with him when the world of sense is shut out as it were for a time, and the soul can soar freely to higher things. But the close of the treatise lapses into disappointing puerilities. Synesius was always more of an author, more of a stylist than a philosopher, but it is strange that he should regard this converse with the divine as mainly useful from a literary point of view. The forecasting of the future pales into insignificance as compared with the choice of an epithet or the turning of a trope; and the main use of dreams, it would seem, is to furnish material for essays. (154) But after all, the fault of Synesius is the fault of his age more than of the man himself. Only, in estimating his philosophy we cannot omit this tendency which reveals a real shallowness of mind, the weakness of a writer who thought more of diction than of philosophic truth.

The Ethics of Synesius. The ethics of Synesius are simply the outcome of his metaphysical system. The gulf which separated God from the world of sense is only reproduced in the moral world by the absolute distinction of the philosopher from the common herd. The destiny of man finds fulfilment in ecstatic union with God. True, but only the man of ease and means who can afford to hold aloof from the defilement of earthly intercourse can hope to attain. And thus we find in Synesius, as the natural result of an Ideal philosophy which required wealth and leisure for its pursuit, a distinct touch of Epicureanism. It is true that he rises in theory above the things of earth, that he despises the honours of the world, and is ready to give up all for union with God; yet his constant prayer to God is that he may enjoy not merely the *mens sana in corpore sano*, but an exemption from all sickness and every temporal affliction, a life of placid and unbroken calm.* He desires neither excessive wealth nor degrading poverty, but only such a competence as will enable him to withdraw from active life, and raise his spirit far above its material surroundings.† "I could wish that it "were possible for our nature always to be bent on con- "templation,"‡ says Synesius; and again, "the life according "to reason is the true end of man."‖ Action of whatever

---

* H. III., 380-390, and 510-524. Cf. V., 40, and VI., 29 to the end.
† H. I., 29-32.

> ἐμι δ' ἀψόφητον εἴη
> βιόταν ἄσημον ἕλκειν,
> τὰ μὲν εἰς ἄλλους ἄσημον
> τὰ δὲ πρὸς θεὸν ἰιδότα.

‡ *Dion*, p. 47.
‖ Ep. 136.

nature is a sign of weakness, a degradation to which we submit unwillingly, and only of necessity ; and Synesius, in *The Dion*, even speaks admiringly of the hermits of the Thebaid,* or rather sympathises with their retirement from the world and envies them their opportunities for silent communion and exalted thought.†

Such a religion as this carried in it the germs of failure: Religious it reminds one in its exclusiveness, of the glimpse of heaven Exclusiveness. given by Proteus in the *Odyssey*‡ "where life is easiest for "men ; nor is snow there, nor storm, nor any rain, but "ocean ever sendeth forth the breeze of the shrill west to "blow cool on men." But only the kinsmen of the Gods pass after death to those abodes of bliss : the rest of men may roam for ever disconsolate in the gloom of Hades.

And though we must not forget that asceticism was a feature of the age, and that Christianity had its monks and anchorites—who withdrew from the corrupt life of the great cities and left the crowd to sink unchecked by holier influence to lower depths of sin—still with Christianity there was a difference. Asceticism went on side by side with the growth of the Church ; it was but one aspect of the Christian life of the age. In Neo-Platonism, the principle of religion for the philosopher only is paramount always, until the common brotherhood of humanity is lost sight of, and the divine is practically only allowed to exist in a man so far as he is conscious of its existence in him.||

But there was a deeper source of weakness even than Evil this. If there was one poisonous influence that sapped the consequences of depreciation purity and soundness of Greek life, and hastened the of practical life.

* *Dion.*, p. 45. At the same time his Greek aversion to τὸ βαναυσὸν comes out in his contemptuous allusion to their basket weaving.

† H. III., 51-65, of the solitude of the desert.

‡ *Odyssey*, IV., 563-570.

|| Kingsley. *Alexandria and her Schools*, c. III.

downfall of their greatness, it was the notion that work was meant for slaves, and that literary and philosophic leisure was what befitted a gentleman. Philosophically it led of course to a sharp distinction between the moral and the spiritual. Virtue is not the end, it is only the means to an end.* Its real value is as a καθαρσις, a purification : and it is thus a necessary preparation for the contemplative life. It is easy, however, to see how such an estimate of virtue might open the door to downright immorality.† The next step after reducing virtue to this humble rôle is to deny its necessity altogether. Once let the philosopher attain, by a spiritual effort, to ecstatic union, and virtue becomes useless to him : a dangerous doctrine for society at large.

The essential thing is not, as the popular belief implies, to live an honest life ;‡ and to regard that as the end of our efforts is to confound the means with the end. Without reason there is no virtue, or rather reason is the only virtue. For it is by the intellect alone that we hold intercourse with God. The mind is the true temple of God. In it he resides when he descends to commune with us.||

Virtue's function is to purify the temple, and by purging the mind of all terrestial pollutions to fit it for the Divine visitation. It is not enough to shake ourselves free from the taint of matter,§ for negative goodness is at best a makeshift. We must develope the divine within us that we may become God.¶

---

* Tillemont, vol. xii., p. 501.

† v. Ueberweg. Philos., vol. i., p. 289. The Gnostic is saved without works like a spiritual man. This doctrine was used by Marcus and his followers as an excuse for immorality and sexual excesses (Iren. I., 13).

‡ Ep. 136.

|| *Dion*, p. 49.

§ *Dion*, p. 50.

¶ H. I., 128 to end.

All these doctrines are stated and the deductions from Synesius' practice better than his theories. them drawn, in various passages scattered through the writings of Synesius. But it would not be fair to close this sketch of his philosophy without adding that he was infinitely above his creed in many ways (he would have said "below")—and fortunately for mankind and Cyrene, did not by any means practise rigorously what he preached.

He sympathises with the ascetic tendency, but he can enjoy the delights of a sportsman without scruple. Pleasure, he even says, was given by God as the clasp (περόνη) which enables the soul to endure the contiguity of the body;[*] and in the same work:—"I know that I am human and "neither a God that I should be averse to every pleasure; "nor yet a beast that I should delight in mere sensual "enjoyment."[†] It is this sanity of reason, this healthy practical tone which is the salt of Synesius' character and saves him from falling into the excesses to which his views would seem to lead him.

Lastly, though his philosophy contemned the practical life and would have fain affected indifference to all human interests, Synesius was never prevented for a moment by these tenets from devoting himself to the cause of mankind. His very reluctance, which appears again and again in his letters, a kind of mournful resignation to a fate which forced him to leave meditation for the strife of war, for the business of life,—this very reluctance, I say, enhances the merit of his sacrifice.

Born to an independence, brought up to a quiet, studious life, he yet never forgot his duty as a citizen to his country, and in her cause he was always ready to give up his books and the leisure he loved so well, and

[*] *Dion*, 45.
[†] *Dion*, 47.

whether as ambassador, or soldier, or bishop to serve
Cyrene with the devotion of a true patriot.

view of   In conclusion, it will not be amiss, to quote from the
De Providentia a striking passage which has a peculiar
significance, when we consider how deeply Synesius' whole
life was affected by his surroundings, and how, contrary
to his own inclinations and notions of what was best, he
submitted always to the call of duty as to the voice of God.

"For every life is a potentiality of virtue, and God
"and Fortune have assigned to us as actors rôles in the
"great world drama. Nor is one life in any way better
"or worse than another. Each uses his opportunities as
"best he can; and the actor who deserves ridicule is
"only he who declines his part and prefers a different one.
" . . . . The true mark of boorishness is to be
"impatient in waiting for the life God gives us. Just
"as an ill-bred guest at a feast importunes to be helped
"before his turn."*

HOW FAR WAS SYNESIUS A SOPHIST?

Two writings of Synesius remain for discussion, the
Dion and the *Calvitii Encomium*, neither of which can be
fairly classed among his philosophical works. It is true
they both contain allusions to his philosophical creed, but
their interest apart from this is wholly biographical and
literary. From the former point of view some reference
has already been made to them, but the literary side has
not yet been touched upon, and as it is important in helping
us to form a true estimate of Synesius' philosophy, I have
appended this sketch of *The Dion* to the section in which
that philosophy is discussed.

* *De Providentia*, p. 106.

During his stay at Alexandria Synesius seems to have made enemies among the class of the sophists, the professional teachers of rhetoric and *belles-lettres,* who were very probably, as he says, shallow thinkers, men whose art lay in the manipulation of words and whose aim was not to find truth but to win the applause of their audience. It is easy to see how ill feeling would arise. The Neo-Platonist, proud of his monopoly in esoteric truth, would repeat with an air of intense superiority the tirades of Plato against the sophists of his own day; and the old Greek feeling of contempt for a paid teacher was still strong enough to establish a caste of unremunerated wisdom. The sophists, indignant at Synesius' pretensions, turned on him with a *tu quoque* and in so many words claimed him as one of themselves. Such we may safely infer to have been the nature of their charge, although the statement (in Ep. 153) to Hypatia is less explicit. " I have been reproached," he says, " with sacrificing "philosophy to literature, with paying too much attention "to style, and with wasting on the production of ephemeral "verses the time which I might have devoted to more worthy "objects."

His defence is ingenious. He resorts to a compromise and defends the pursuit of literature as an amusement. At the same time he cleverly shields himself by the example of a representative sophist, Dion Chrysostom, whose name this treatise bears and whose reputation his adversaries would be bound to respect. Dion Chrysostom* was a man of character and ability, but his works, though famous in

---

* As a politician he constituted himself the mentor of states and sovereigns and seems to have spoken out with great boldness on the abuses of his age. During his exile among the Getae he lived a simple monastic life, digging and planting his plot of ground and paying occasional visits to the neighbouring camp. On the death of Domitian he quelled a military disturbance by his eloquence, and enjoyed the unbounded respect of the Emperor Trajan. *De Dione ex Philostrato.* Migne. Introd. to *The Dion.*

their day, were the product of an age of literary imitation and barrenness of thought. His intellectual activity had two distinct periods, and while in the first Synesius, in opposition to Philostratus, regards Dion as an unmitigated sophist, on the ground of his fierce tirades against Socrates and philosophers in general, he holds that a time came when he deserted sophistry for the art of πολιτική and won a right to the title of philosopher. He by no means, however, neglected letters, and the writings which belong to this later period of his life are " models of natural writing and " simple elegance."

Such was the man whom Synesius set up as his model, and it is interesting to trace even in the titles of his works an almost servile adherence to his master's example.

Abstract of The Dion.

To return, however, to the main argument. The mind cannot endure a constant state of tension, it must have relaxation, and what nobler form of relaxation can be found than the pursuit of letters? Philosophy is not to be attaind *per saltum.* (42) Literature forms the best introduction to it, and is in fact the necessary preparation for the higher science.

The true philosopher must be a man of universal culture, and true philosophy ought to combine the gifts of all the muses. Other men may specialize, but the philosopher, like a true eclectic, is the devotee of all arts and sciences ; and while through philosophy he enjoys communion with God, he needs (43) the medium of rhetoric and poetry, faculties subordinate to true reason, in his intercourse with the uninitiated crowd. From this point of view such pursuits are by no means to be despised by the philosopher : and it is only the carping critics who slight them because they lack themselves the art of expression. (44) Philosophy is after all only for the few, but let us grant to the uninitiated admission to the vestibule of the temple which they may not enter, let us throw off literary trifles for the amusement of outsiders and divert them by the artifices of language from any intrusion on the domain of incommunicable truth.

(45) There is another aspect of the question which concerns the philosopher more nearly. So weak is human nature that it cannot remain long in contemplation of absolute truth. We need recreation : and what more harmless than the relief which letters afford ? Be sure that if a man cannot enjoy these innocent pleasures, he will find in sensual gratification the diversion he requires.

(46) Synesius then alludes to the ascetics, the monks of the desert, for whom the sophists of Alexandria must have felt unqualified contempt. He recognizes in their solitary, thrifty life, the principle of a truly philosophic endeavour to emancipate the soul from matter and raise it to communion with God. At the same time he pours scorn on their basket-weaving, in spite of his admission that recreation is a necessity: and the whole point of the allusion lies in the argument for the ideal life of pure contemplation which the Neo-Platonists so consistently harped upon. The three sections which follow are mainly taken up with the discussion of ethical and philosophical questions, which have been already treated of and may be passed over here. To return to his onslaught on the sophists. (51) "What can be more pitiable," Synesius asks, "than the sorry plight of those aspirants to philosophy, who "pursue her irrationally and without proper training. Rams "would succeed as well, if they turned their attention to "the subject."

(52) The fact is that the sophists should rest content with the elementary principles of philosophy : and holding the middle ground between ἀμαθία and σοφία, make right opinion their goal, leaving higher matters to those who

are more capable. Instead of this, the sophists, more reckless than the angels, are so far from imitating the modesty of Socrates, that they fling themselves into an abyss by tampering with esoteric truths beyond their ken, losing thereby the praise which is due to the respectful crowd who do not interfere, and bringing on themselves the condemnation of that helpless ignorance which ignores its own existence.

(53) It is this attempt to trespass beyond one's proper sphere, to outstep the limitations of one's intellect, that Synesius inveighs against. A purely literary turn of mind deserves praise as such, but only in so far as it does not tamper with philosophy, before going through the necessary propaedeutic training.

(54) Happy the man to whom the Gods have granted the double gift of eloquence and philosophy.

Then follows a satirical passage, which recalls the famous contrast of the philosopher and the man of the world in Plato's *Theaetetus*. The sophist is the public slave in so far as it is his business to be entertaining. He must speak whether ill or well, and make the most of himself and his voice by art and nature.

(55) Synesius, on the other hand, expatiates very ungraciously on his own independence and freedom from such servile restrictions. He can choose his own time and place and he has no audience to flatter. "I can sing to myself," he says, "for hours together, while the stream beside me flows on its course, with no measured drip like the water-clock at whose mercy the sophist lies."

(56) Again he censures their verbal facility, their readiness to discourse on any theme proposed, their neglect of matter in the pursuit of style, the substitution, in short, of words for thoughts. What, too, can be more contemptible than their canvassing for disciples and the mutual jealousies to which such rivalries give rise?

Or what can be more absurd than the pretensions of such men to learning, the assumption of infallibility which leads them to scorn any opinions but their own?

(57) They might have taken a lesson in humility from the old philosophers—Socrates attended the lectures of Prodicus, Hippias and Protagoras: Aspasia even gave him instruction; nor was he ashamed to enter into conversation and to argue on equal terms with any man he chanced to meet.

(59D) But there is a second charge which Synesius feels called upon to rebut. Certain bibliophiles, a class of connoisseurs not unknown at Alexandria, had reproached Synesius with having, in his library, incorrect and faulty texts, not a few. Synesius laughs at the notion. What matter is it whether one syllable is put for another, so long as the sense is not obscured? A man should read with the mind rather than the eye. Nay the very necessity of emendation is in itself an excellent training. This leads up to a very boastful description of Synesius' power as an improvisatore—the whole passage in fact to the conclusion of the treatise shows up the weak side of Synesius' character; a self-satisfaction and vanity, confined it is true almost entirely to literary matters, but still a great weakness and one that his enemies would not fail to take advantage of.

The wonderful facility which he possessed of adapting himself to the styles of different writers of every age has been already touched upon; and in a society where superficial cleverness could always win applause, it was not unnatural that a man with any tendency to vanity—and what Greek was wholly free from such?—should let himself be carried away first to make a display and then a boast of his ability.

(62) "Often," he says, "when I am reading a book I "pay no attention to what the author is going to say, but I

"raise my eyes, and, under the inspiration of the moment,
"I compose the sequel to what I have been reading without
"hesitation, thus frequently anticipating not simply the
"ideas but the actual words of the author. I remember,
"too, occasions when finding myself in the company of
"others, and being asked to read aloud from the work of
"some distinguished writer, if the opportunity presented
"itself, I would add some passage of my own invention,
"and that without effort—I call the God of Eloquence to
"witness—but simply by giving free play to my imagination
"and my tongue. Presently arose a murmur of approval,
"bursting forth into applause in compliment to the author
"of the book, but unconsciously rather to my inter-
"polations."

It is a sad fall from the Empyrean heights of Neo-
Platonism; but we cannot ignore in Synesius what was
after all the fault of his age, and the necessary outcome of
the society in which he moved. Only why this intense
bitterness against the sophists? May not Synesius in his
heart of hearts have felt a lurking suspicion that his own
genius was by no means free from the taint of so-called
sophistry, and that this literary trifling, of which he is so
unpardonably vain, was little better than the word-play or
empty rhetoric he so unsparingly condemns in others?
Was not the real difference at bottom simply this: that
Synesius made an amusement of what with the sophists
was necessarily a trade?* A brief consideration of the
Calvitii Encomium will I think bear out this view. It does
not matter in the least whether this work be a satire on
the sophists or an unconscious imitation of their style—in
either case no object could be served by its production; it
is too pedantic to be amusing, and amazement at the

---

* Cf. the phrase of Constant Martha, "un sophiste amateur."

ingenuity of the writer who marshals every branch of learning on the side of his cause is qualified by disgust at the waste of time involved in even a cursory pérusal. The *raison d'être* of its composition is thoroughly Alexandrine. Dion Chrysostom had frittered away his energies in a *Comae Encomium*. Synesius, who was prematurely bald, is only too eager to enter the lists against the typical sophist whose works he so admired, and the present *jeu d'esprit* is the result.

It would be at once tedious and unprofitable to attempt an abstract of this work. Arguments are adduced in favour of baldness, from agriculture, astronomy, medicine, history and philosophy. The three hundred Spartans who combed their long hair in the pass of Thermopylæ are contrasted with the soldiers of Alexander the Great, who shaved because they found their beards gave an advantage to the enemy. Of course Homer is pressed into the service and the fact that Athene laid hold of the locks of * Achilles from behind, is adduced as a proof that he was already bald in front.

But enough has been said to give some notion of the nature of the subject and Synesius' method of treating it. It is worth noticing that his language at the conclusion precludes the notion of the whole piece being a skit or satire. On the contrary he is rather proud of his performance and in a letter to Pylaemenes † says, " this book, "composed in accordance with Attic taste, has cost me "considerable care: if however it wins the approbation of " Pylaemenes that is enough to commend it to posterity."

" L'art de bien dire," to use a phrase of Druon's, was the curse of the Alexandrine age, and the Society which laid

* Iliad, I., 197.
† Ep. 74.

such stress on rhetorical smartness created the demand
which the much-abused sophists lived to supply.

It would have been strange if Synesius had altogether
escaped the infection. That he did not so escape is clear,
and we must not leave out of sight, in estimating his
philosophy, the tendency to literary cleverness for its own
sake, which he indulged in as a recreation from the pursuit
of severer studies.

Such a spirit of literary dilettanteism is not compatible
with true philosophy, and Synesius, in spite of his pretensions, does not wholly escape the censure which he
passes on the sophists of the day. In conclusion it is only
fair to state that the *Calvitii Encomium* is certainly an*
earlier work than *The Dion*, and was probably written soon
after the return from Constantinople. It is, moreover, the
only work of the kind which Synesius has left us.
Fortunately for his own sake, a more useful sphere of
labour was destined to absorb him, and direct his energies
to more practical purpose in the service of mankind.

---

* Druon (Note 2, page 259), argues as follows :—

    (i.) Synesius sends his book to his friends at Constantinople. It was
        written therefore after 400.

    (ii.) He does not refer to it in any letters to his friends at Alexandria ;
        he was therefore probably in that city.

    (iii.) *The Dion* censures the very type of work to which this belongs ;
        moreover one can understand how it might easily give a handle
        to the sophists, to whose attacks *The Dion* is a reply.

HIS

RELATION TO CHRISTIANITY.

"ὅτι πολιτικὴν ἀρετὴν ἱερωσύνῃ συνάπτειν τὸ κλώθειν ἐστὶ τὰ ἀσύγκλωστα."

H

HIS RELATIONSHIP TO CHRISTIANITY.

IT is with no intention of severing the religion of Synesius from his philosophy that I have treated under separate heads of his Neo-Platonic theories and the Christian development which they underwent. The two are inseparably connected, and as there is nothing more hollow than a so-called philosophy which slights morality and shelves religious feeling, so there are few things more unstable and unreal than a religion based solely on unthinking faith and the accumulated force of custom. Religion can never be long divorced from philosophy: we must have an emotional sense developed, but it must be tempered by reason; we must have a well-trained reason, but it needs the warming glow of moral enthusiasm.

There was no danger of such separation in the third century of the Christian era; Neo-Platonism was in its prime, and the century which saw the development of the Oriental and Hellenic tendencies into a systematized philosophy in the great work of Plotinus, witnessed also the first attempt to systematize Christian dogma in the writings of Origen. *Relations of Religion and Philosophy in 3rd Century A.D.*

The two schools were for some time on friendly terms, for there was a spirit of tolerance on both sides. Clement could recognize the seed of the Divine Λόγος as implanted in the Greek philosophers, and could speak of Plato in terms of real respect and reverence,* The Neo-Platonists *Clement and Plotinus.*

* *Paed.* III., 11. *Strom.* V., 8. V. Ueberweg. *Hist. of Philos.*, Vol. I., p. 314.

on their side, from a no less lofty standpoint, could patronize the school of Christian Gnosis, and acknowledge the elements of what they regarded as popular truth, while they would notice with some self-satisfaction the points in which the Christian doctrine seemed to converge and harmonize with their own views. A more important tendency towards reconciliation lay deeper still, for the problem which both schools were trying to solve was one and the same. Theology was at the basis of either system, and the feeling of alienation from God, the yearning for a higher revelation and a closer union with God, called into existence the Neo-Platonists and the Jewish Alexandrine schools side by side with the Christian Church, whose founder had given the answer to the problem in his own life and person nigh three hundred years before.

The position then at this period was briefly as follows:— **Platonic influence at work in both Systems.** The Neo-Platonists were working out their religion on Platonic lines, while at the same time susceptible to the influence of Eastern mysticism.

The Alexandrine Fathers were developing Christian doctrine by the light of Hellenic culture, and if not quite on Platonic lines, at all events under Platonic influence. To mention very summarily a few points of agreement between the opposing systems. The Divine Word which, from the time of Philo onwards, plays so important a part in all theologies, according to Clement and Plotinus, enlightens the souls of men from the beginning.* The Platonic distinction between ethic and dianoetic virtue, and the consequent importance of philosophy is plainly recognised in the statement that whoever will attain to knowledge without dialectic and the study of nature, is like a man who expects to gather grapes without cultivating the vine.†

* *Strom.* V., 3.
† *Str.* I. 9.

Man must rise through the world of γένεσις and sin,[*] to communion with God ; and so with the Neo-Platonist, he must shake himself free from the thraldom of matter and strive to attain that ecstatic union when " we are laid asleep " in body, and become a living soul."

Both Clement and Plotinus regarded a positive knowledge of God as impossible—we know only what God is not. Both held a doctrine of a Trinity, and how closely the two doctrines were allied, has been shown in the preceding chapter.

The real and essential difference, however between the two systems lay in this, that while the Neo-Platonists could only conceive a religion for the philosopher, and like a true aristocracy of intellect kept " the kernel of the nut for them- " selves and gave even the husks grudgingly to the mob so " far beneath them, Christianity was still true to the wider " principle of humanity, which has always been its deepest " source of strength and vitality."[†]   And so without repressing the free play of the intellect the Christian philosophers made no monopoly to themselves of esoteric truth, but taking their stand on the moral as well as on the intellectual ground they recognized frankly as a reality what with the Neo-Platonists was an unwelcome and half-suppressed belief that there is in the lowest of men an inward conscience, a germ of pure reason, a hope of something more divine, which, however dimmed or crushed, is capable of being awakened and purified to become the groundwork of a higher life.

Such was the relation of Greek and Christian thought in the third century, and in spite of real differences, a reconciliation between the two would undoubtedly have been only the work of time and the sequel of their parallel

Essential differences between Neo-Platonism and Christianity.

---

[*] *Str.* VI., 16.
[†] Kingsley. *Alex. and her Schools.* C. IV.

development. But it was not to be. External causes triumphed over the tendencies of philosophy and nipped its evolution in the bud.

The later Neo-Platonists fell sadly away from the ideal of their predecessors. They passed more and more under the influence of Oriental mysticism, and at the beginning of the fourth century we find philosophy on the decline, and Iamblichus putting magic and theurgy in the place of the ethical and intellectual effort by which, according to the earlier Neo-Platonists the soul might rise to the vision of the Gods. And so free thought declined, became in fact almost extinct ; and the age of dogmatism arose, and men appealed to the *ipse dixit* of Plato or Aristotle, forgetting in their self-contentment to attempt the working out of their own salvation, mental or spiritual. The end was well nigh come.

Decline of free thought.

And strangely enough, Christianity too fell away from its ideal, though through a different cause. The Church was organized by Constantine for political ends : and it was clearly a gain to the Church as an institution to be so organised. But while the spoils of the Pagan temples enriched the rising Church, and while her Bishops became the most influential men in city, town, and province, there was a distinct retrogression in morality, and the Church lost that simplicity, purity, and self-sacrifice which had marked the era of her depression and apparent weakness.* The records of the age teem with instances of the ambition and rivalry of the bishops. The high offices of the Church became prizes to unscrupulous aspirants to power, and their schisms and intrigues, the want of charity, the hardness and positive cruelty which were the invariable accompaniments of General Councils—all these things hurt the Christian Ideal and insensibly modified human

Growing power of the Church.

* Allen's *Continuity of Christian Thought*, pp. 132, 133.

convictions about the character of God and his relations to mankind.

It is not surprising after this if the Church, as a vast political organisation, forgot or disdained the need of philosophic development and fell into the dogmatic tendency which was already sapping the strength of the Hellenic schools. Nor further is there need of elaborate demonstration to show that the union between Greek and Christian thought, which seemed probable in an age when both were advancing side by side with all the vigour of originality to aid in their evolution, was absolutely hopeless when once dogmatism had come in to stereotype and to sever.

Synesius was thus born into an age when Christianity Difficulties in presented least attraction to the Philosophic mind. External the way of Synesius' pomp and ritual, growing power and influence it possessed conversion. in no slight measure; but the thoughtful mind could not but be repelled by the violence and jealousy of some of its prelates, could not restrain a doubt as to the efficacy of its work among the degraded city populace of that corrupt and vicious age.

Moreover, there was a natural jealousy between the representatives of the old philosophy and the new religion which threatened to supplant them. As Zeller puts it, "step by step, Greece lost her intellectual prestige and "the last remaining fragments were torn from her grasp by "the victory of Christianity." Neo-Platonism represents her despairing attempt to rescue the forms of Greek culture from her mighty rival.

One more cause of alienation lay undoubtedly in the Catholic reception by the Church of all Nationalities and especially of the Goths, those outer barbarians who had already commenced to overrun the Roman empire. To Hypatia the mere fact of a Goth or Hun becoming a

Christian must have stamped the religion in her mind as one for savages. The old race feeling was aroused and undoubtedly lay at the root of Synesius' hostility to the Arian heresy so prevalent among the Goths ; a hostility that appears in the *De Providentia*, which was written some years before the probable date of his conversion to Christianity.

Into this school of thought, Synesius was plunged at the most impressionable age, and its influence upon him must not be underrated in emphasizing a point which has been generally rather overlooked, I mean the difficulty which lay in the way of his conversion.

The Church had few attractions for a Philosopher. To sum up briefly : Synesius lived at a time when the Church had more attractions for the ambitious man than for the philosopher. He was a Greek to the backbone, and would feel an *a priori* contempt for the religion of barbarians. Lastly the early influences of his life must have been antagonistic to Christianity, and the impression of the Church which he would get in Alexandria, with its brutal mob and its unscrupulous prelate, was not calculated to dispose him favourably towards its doctrines. Possibly he saw a better side of Christianity in his native town of Cyrene, but this is mere conjecture, and we can only guess at the motives which led Synesius to adopt the Christian faith.

Synesius Relation to Christianity. Our present purpose is rather to establish his actual relations to that faith, and in discussing this question I shall treat of these relations under the following heads.

(i.) Synesius' declared dissent.

(ii.) His official Christianity—(*a*) as seen in his language as Bishop. (*b*) as seen in his acts as Bishop.

(iii.) Internal evidence as to his belief.

(i.) Synesius' declared dissent :—

His declared dissent. The points on which Synesius found his philosophy at variance with the popular Christianity (τοῖς θρυλλουμένοις) are three in number, and are stated very clearly in the letter to his brother Evoptius. That his scruples should have been limited to these three doctrines is certainly remarkable, but while on the one hand the letter is too explicit to admit of Kraus' suggestion that Synesius' acquaintance with Christianity was fragmentary and incomplete ; still less must we listen to Clausen's theory that he was intentionally silent on the more important points, and that this explains the absence of any reservations affecting the birth of Christ.*

To do this is to misunderstand altogether Synesius' character, to attribute to him a duplicity of which he was incapable. And after all the explanation is not far to seek. The key to it lies in the point that with Synesius it was philosophy that was at stake ; he might modify his old theories, but he declined to abandon them, and the hope that he expresses in a letter written soon after his conversion shows that he wished his new religion not to involve a departure from, but a rising to philosophy. Clearly then the points he urges are those which clashed with his convictions; points which as popular doctrines were the topic of every preacher, and must often have recurred in the conversation of daily life. If on other points than these, Synesius is silent, we may assume, I think, fairly, that he had found himself able to harmonise the truths they conveyed with his own philosophy.

To deal with the points in order. ἀμέλει τὴν ψυχήν οὐκ ἀξιώσω πότε σώματος ὑστερογένη νουίζειν.

The pre-existence of the soul.

Here Synesius had certainly all the array of ancient thought and learning on his side. No Idealist could entertain for a moment the belief that matter was prior to spirit : and it is hard to imagine that any Christian

* Tub. Q. for 1865, p. 546.

philosopher can have held this view. Possibly the popular notion sprang out of the controversies of the time. For example, the question as to the Divinity of Christ was solved by certain schools on the assumption that the Divine nature entered into our Lord after birth—and such a notion might easily be strained to support the posterior creation of the soul to the body. But with the Neo-Platonist, soul was eternal, immortality belonged to it before and will belong to it after its earthly career. The body is a mere tenement, an accident in the life of the soul, apart from which it has no real existence. Synesius, however, need not have appealed to the old philosophers for support in this view. The doctrine of the Divine Λόγος, eternal as God himself, was no new one, and the belief that the Divine element, the soul within us, sprang from this eternal source of life and existence, carried with it the necessity for the pre-existence of soul *qua* soul. Nay, Origen expressly affirms the very doctrine which Synesius holds out for.

The eternity of the world. The second point (οὔτε τὸν κόσμον συνδιαφθείρεσθαι...) practically turns on the same question, the eternity of soul. For this involves the consequent eternity of matter not *qua* matter, but as the emanation of soul and the necessary vehicle for the soul's actualization. Here again Origen is with Synesius as far as the eternal creation of the world is concerned. He says, "the creation of the world cannot "have begun in any given moment of time, but must be "conceived of as without beginning."* The world, however, is subject to decay, and the duration of each world-aeon is limited. But while the school of Christian Gnosis advanced no definite theories as to the destruction of the world, it is obvious from the apostolic writings how prominent a part this notion of the speedy end of all things played in the

* Or. *De Princip.* III., 303.

popular mind. Synesius' philosophic position then on this point may be best summed up in the words of Plotinus: ἐπεί οὐκ ἦν ὅτε οὐκ ἐψυχοῦτο τόδε τὸ πᾶν, οὐδ' ἐνῆν ὅτε σῶμα ὑφειστήκει ψυχῆς ἀπούσης, οὐδὲ ὕλη πότε ὅτ' ἀκόσμητος ἦν... σώματος μὴ ὄντος οὐκ ἂν προέλθοι ψυχή.* It was this close interconnection between soul and matter, this necessity of matter as the ὄχημα ψυχῆς that led the Neo-Platonists to a virtual assertion of the eternity of matter itself.

The last point is more important—τὴν καθωμιλημένην The doctrine ἀνάστασιν ἱερόν τι καὶ ἀπόρρητον ἡγοῦμαι καὶ πολλοῦ δέω of the ταῖς τοῦ πλήθους ὑπολήψεσιν ὁμολογῆσαι—and like the other Resurrection. two it turns on a question connected with the soul, for undoubtedly the point at issue in Synesius' mind was this— is there such a thing as Individual Immortality? That was the wider issue, but there was a narrower question involved in it. The Church showed a growing tendency to the grossest material notions as to the nature of the resur- rection body. The Anthropomorphists of the age insisted on the literal interpretation of the raising of the dead, and Theophilus was only the forerunner of an era in which Origen and his followers were regarded as heretical and their views denounced accordingly. The opposing views stood thus :—While Origen held the notion of a glorified resurrection body, Jerome and the extreme exponents of the sensuous doctrine insisted on the literal and actual restoration of our earthly bodies even to teeth, nails, and hair. (The γναθμὸς ὀδόντων of the damned makes this assumption necessary.)† Of course Synesius was not likely to give a moment's thought to such corporeal fancies, but the question of Individual Immortality was a much graver one, and after all it is the essential point, whatever our notions may be, as Christians, of the future life. Nor is the

* Plot. *Enn.*, IV., 3, 9.
† Hagenbach, *History of Christian Doctrines*, Vol. II., p. 91.

resurrection body anything more than a material expression of the spiritual truth which as Christians we believe.

To a Neo-Platonist the soul was immortal, it is true, but as we have no recollection of the individual lives we have already past through, so the πόμα ληθαῖον of which we drink at the parting of soul and body secures to us in the future a similar oblivion of the past. Our soul may rise to the stars or to the region of pure thought, or it may pass into a fresh human body, or, if it has misused its opportunities, into the form of some lower animal ; still by toil and purifying fire it can rise from its degradation and attain at last, to what ? union with the Divine, a merging in the world soul from whence it sprang—the attainment of the Buddhist Nirvana. The half-suggested query of Plotinus as to the soul's pre-existence shows what its future might be expected to prove.* ἡμεῖς δὲ, τίνες δὲ ἡμεῖς ; — ἢ καὶ πρὸ τοῦ ταύτην τὴν γένεσιν γενέσθαι ἦμεν ἐκεῖ ἄνθρωποι, ἄλλοι ὄντες, καί τινες καὶ θεοί. ψυχαὶ καθαραὶ καὶ νοῦς συνημμένος τῇ ἁπάσῃ οὐσίᾳ, μέρη ὄντες τοῦ νοητοῦ, οὐκ ἀφωρισμένα οὐδ᾽ ἀποτετμημένα, ἀλλ᾽ ὄντες τοῦ ὅλου.

What, however, was Synesius' attitude to the Christian doctrine ? His language is too brief and general for any accurate inference. " I regard it as a sacred and unspeakable " truth." This is high praise from a Neo-Platonist. May not Synesius have felt the importance of the theory of individual immortality as a moral lever, a stimulus to right action, and an explanation of the imperfections, the half-developed faculties and aspirations with which man closes his life on earth.

So far, we have had to deal with actual points of difference. We come next to a difference in principle, which affects Synesius' whole attitude to Christianity. After

* Plot. Enn., VI., 4, 14.

stating the three main doctrines which he could not bring himself to accept, he appends the following statement of his views on popular religion:—

"The philosophic mind while it makes truth the object His views on popular Religion.
"of its contemplation, concedes the necessity of fiction.
"For light stands to the eye in the same relation as truth to
"the people, and just as too much light only blinds us, so I
"hold that fiction is profitable for the people, and that truth
"is harmful to those who cannot fix their gaze upon the
"brightness of what truly *is*. If therefore I can be bishop
"on these terms, philosophizing at home, and speaking in
"parables (myths) abroad, I accept the office. I shall not
"teach, but I will not undo the teaching of my predecessors.
"There shall be no disguise—I have no intention of feigning
"dogmatism. What have the people to do with philosophy?
"Divine truth must be and is rightly an unspeakable
"mystery."

This language at first reading jars on our notions of Christianity and the duties of a preacher of the Gospel, and it is right that it should call forth a protest in so far as it represents the exclusiveness of a Neo-Platonist. So long as the philosopher regards the common herd with pitying contempt, and reserves to himself the truths which he holds to be beyond their comprehension, he is enfeebling the nobler side of his nature, and stifling the sympathy that he owes as a man to his fellow-men. This was the fatal weakness, as we have seen, of Neo-Platonism and in so far as Synesius is actuated here by the selfish aristocratic pride of his philosophy, no censure can be too severe.

But there is another side to the question. There must There is a true and a false Esotericism. always have been, must always be, an esoteric and an exoteric religion. Men are not equal in force of intellect any more than in fortune. Each man can only see what he has eyes to see. "He that hath ears to hear let him hear," proclaims the relativity of religious truth. No two thinking men look at a doctrine in precisely the same way; there is a shade of meaning more or less in the view each takes of it. There is something in one man's past experience that makes him susceptible to an appeal, and the absence of that something may make the same appeal meaningless to another.

That the Christian school of Alexandria recognized this distinction is evident from Clement's view that we need the aid of philosophy in order to advance from faith to knowledge—and the same writer compares the gnostic to him who believes without knowing, as the grown-up man to the child. But the esoteric beliefs of the Christian Fathers were not fenced round with mystery. A true Christian philosophy never forbids any of its disciples to approach and gaze on its sacred doctrine. Only where there is a danger of shaking the popular faith, of unsettling men's minds by presenting old truths under altered aspects, the teacher of religion will be cautious and pave the way for the acceptance of higher truth, by emphasizing the spiritual meaning that underlies the popular creeds. There is no selfish monopoly of truth in such an esotericism, but a wise reticence based on a careful estimate of the mental calibre of its would-be disciples.

Contrast this with the esoteric selfishness of the Heathen schools. "Their avowed intention and wish was "to leave the herd, as they called them, in the mere outward " observance of the old idolatries, while they themselves, "the cultivated philosophers, had the monoply of those "deeper spiritual truths which were contained under the "old superstitions and were too sacred to be profaned by "the vulgar eye."* Once more then, at the risk of repetition, we must not forget that in turning to Christianity,

* Kingsley, *Alexandria*, C. IV., p. 104.

Synesius did not rid himself wholly of the prejudices of the school in which he had been reared, and, therefore, in so far as his language proclaims the exclusiveness of religion and warns off the *vulgus profanum* from its consecrated ground, Synesius was wrong.

In concluding the consideration of Synesius' proclaimed dissent it is worth while, in view of a note of Gibbon,* to point out that Synesius' use of the word "myth" does not imply any necessary contempt. Gibbon's words are "He refused to preach *fables* to the people, "unless he might be permitted to philosophize at home." The whole tone of the note is misleading, and the term "fables" thus introduced without note or comment is especially so. Synesius' own words at the outset of the *De Providentia* are very much in point here. He speaks of the young Osiris as φιλήκοος καὶ φιλόμυθος, and then adds ὁ γὰρ μῦθος φιλοσόφημα παίδων ἐστιν,† surely no depreciatory view this of μῦθος, as the graphic form under which a deeper meaning is conveyed to the childish mind. And if, as is most likely the case, Synesius is recalling the earlier books of Plato's republic, where he sketches out his scheme of education, what can be more pure or beautiful than the myths he contemplates for boyhood, which shall present God to a child as the giver of Good only, and purify the divine of all the earthly taints which sully the old-world stories.

(ii.) Synesius' official Christianity :—(a) As seen in his language.—That Synesius was very imperfectly acquainted with the Scriptures at the time of his appointment appears from the closing words of his first charge as Bishop to Peter the Presbyter. "If I have found nothing to say of a

Margin note: Synesius' use of the phrase φιλομύθων.

---

* Gibbon, Vol. II., C. XX., p. 179.
† *De Prov.*, 90.

"character familiar to your ears, you must make allowance
"for me, and lay the blame at your own doors for having
"chosen in preference to those who know the oracles of
"God one who is ignorant of them."*

Synesius must however have devoted himself to the
study of the Jewish Scriptures during the seven months'
delay that intervened between his election and consecration,
for we find him quoting scripture loosely but effectively in
the letters which belong to the first year of his episcopate.
Probably his aptitude for picking up the style of an author,
which he rather plumed himself upon,† helped him here.
At the same time his facile memory must have tended to
superficiality which the exaltation of the spirit above the
letter does not wholly palliate. An example will make this
clear. The letter or speech against Andronicus‡ opens with
a typical instance. "The powers of evil are the involuntary
"and detested instruments of the Divine purpose." Then he
adds—"For I will raise up a nation against you and you
"shall suffer such and such evils from them: and at last
"he says . . ." Synesius' comment is—"I don't remember
"the exact words, but I affirm that somewhere in the Scrip-
"tures God is represented as speaking to this effect." In
the same letter he refers to the crucifixion. "Man is indeed
"precious, if for his sake Christ was crucified." And again
in the letter‖ in which he refers to the nailing of Andronicus'
edict on the church doors, he alludes to the inscription set
up by the Jews over the cross and contrasts the two. The
sentence of excommunication, moreover, with which the
letter closes contains subtle reminiscences of the Bible

Speech against Andronicus.

The sentence of Excommunication.

* Ep. 13, 174.
† *Dion*, ad fin.
‡ Ep. 57.
‖ Ep. 58, 202, A.

style and thought, although, as Tillemont shows,* it was probably modelled upon contemporary records and possibly not drawn up by Synesius in person.

Enough however has been said to show that Synesius made some progress in the study of the scriptures before his first year of office ran out, and in this connection we may as well speak of the homilies.

The first of the fragments which bears his name is a The First short address directed against the excesses which too often Homily. attended the *Agape*, and disgraced some churches even in Apostolic times.

Synesius urges his flock to fill a cup to God with wine that intoxicates not,† "For our God is wisdom and reason, "and wine that confounds the reason and leads it astray "has nothing to do with the Word. There is an indulgence "befitting God, and an indulgence befitting devils." He then quotes from Psalm lxxv., 8: "For in the hand of the "Lord there is a cup......," and proceeds to interpret it in the fanciful allegorical fashion of the times. The interpretation as such is too far-fetched to be of any value, but the tone of his language and the method he adopts throw a valuable light on his attitude towards the Jewish Scriptures. "The words," he says, "seem ridiculous, but the sense is "not so. God takes no care for the language that he him-"self inspires, and the Divine Spirit despises the minute "accuracy of writing. Do you wish to see the harmony "that exists in discord?" And then Synesius interprets the cup as the λόγος given to men in the Old and New Testaments. "Each separately is a λόγος, but the blending "of the two in one is the consummation of knowledge.

---

* Till., Vol. XII., p. 536. Cette sentence est fort conformée à celle que St. Athanase avoit fulminée environ 40 ans auparavant contre un autre gouverneur.

† Migne, 295 A.

I

"The Old contained the promise, the New τὸν ἀπόστολον
"ἐξήνεγκε. There has been an unbroken succession of
"teachers, first of the Mosaic law, then of the law of Christ.
"It is one and the same spirit that inspired the prophet and
"the apostle. Like some painter, God of old sketched the
"outline and afterwards elaborated the details of know-
"ledge."

Probable Origenistic influences. Allegorical interpretation was a prominent feature of
the Neo-Platonic system, but it is highly probable that
Synesius owed something here to the influence of Origen.
The grasp' of historical continuity, of the oneness of
revelation and inspiration, is clearly a debt to the writings
of the Alexandrine Father. Origen's view[†] was, "that the
"Gospel and the Apostolic epistles stand in no way behind
"the law and the prophets. The Old Testament is un-
"veiled in the New. The Holy Scriptures were inspired
"by God, and contain his word and revelations. The
"allegorical method of interpretation stands to the ordinary
"method as the spiritual to the corporeal."

On the other hand, Synesius' superficial tendency comes
out in the exclamation that the words in themselves mean
nothing : the exclamation of a man who was little versed in
the Scriptures, and in his bewilderment at a symbolism
which he does not understand rushes at the first explanation
that offers, and reconciles the apparently meaningless
nature of the passage with his belief in its Divine
Inspiration, by a theory, to say the least of it, irreverent
and bordering in its tone on flippancy.

The Second Homily. The Second Homily is simply a fragment and is
addressed to the Neophytes on their admission to full
membership in the Church.[*] There is a distinct advance on
the former in ease of expression and reverence of tone in

† Ueberweg, Vol. I., p. 318.
* p. 297 A. Migne.

this short address. Synesius draws the familiar distinction between material and spiritual sunshine, which occurs in more than one of the earlier hymns.* He concludes with these words—"now each one of you is a messenger of God "in this city. Think, as concerning yourselves, of the "words 'living upon earth, yet having our citizenship in "heaven,' and fear lest ye fall from the worthiness of your "high calling; for the pollution that follows after purifica- "tion is hardly blotted out."

There remain for discussion the hymns which were The Hymns. written under obvious Christian influence and were probably in one or two cases subsequent to Synesius' consecration as Bishop of Ptolemais. I have treated of them all here, because the examination of the Christian element in the latest would be incomplete without some allusion to the stages that had preceded. The following passage therefore is rather an excursus on Hymns, V.-X. than part of the consideration of what I have called Synesius' official Christianity.

The earlier hymns, more especially I.-III., which were all written before Synesius' second visit to Alexandria in 403, have been treated of in connection with his pre-Christian philosophy. To the same period must be added Hymn IV., for there is no allusion to Christian doctrine, and the language frequently recalls and in not a few passages reproduces the words of Hymn III.†

To the second period belong Hymns V. (VI.)? and VIII. This classification is of course conjectural and based solely on internal evidence.

---

* H. III., 258. σὺ γὲ φωτοδότας φῶτος νοίρου. Cf. IV., 210-220. δεύτερος ἥλιος.

† Compare.—III. 212 with IV. 117. III. 213 with IV. 120. III. 258 with IV. 239.

Hymn VI.   To take the sixth first. It contains no direct trace whatever of Christian influence, but there appears a growing
tendency to personify the Trinity far more than in
the earlier Hymns. There is no allusion to the monad of
monads, the unity that combines in itself all opposites. On
the other hand the aspect of God is emphasised as working
in the world through the great order of Nature. It is the
Son in fact, the λόγος, the σοφία of the Father, who is
prominent throughout and the allusion in v. 24 to his freeing
mortals from the necessity of death may not improbably be
referred to a Christian source. The Hymn however is in
any case only transitional, and it is certainly to be placed
earlier than the fifth, in which the theme of song is the son of
a spotless virgin, Christ, who in the form of man came
among men to bring the source of light to their darkness.

It is interesting to notice how Synesius works in the
doctrines of Christianity with his philosophical views and
transfers the phraseology of the earlier hymns to the service
of his new religion.

Christ, as the Reason, the word, like the second Person
of the Plotinic trinity, is φῶς παγᾶιον, ὁ κόσμον κτίσας, but
he is also ἀνθρώπων σώτηρ. In his honour all the works
of nature move and have their being. "From thy bosom
"light beams forth, and reason, and soul. Have pity on
"thy daughter (the soul of man) pent in her mortal prison
"house."* Then after expressing a wish that Cyrene and
Sparta might regain their ancient glories, Synesius closes
his prayer with the aspiration so familiar in the earlier
hymns, "that he might enjoy a life of freedom from
"pain and trouble, and through purification from the
"defilement of matter attain to union with the source
"of life." The last lines of the Hymn would seem by

* Cf. H. III. 585-7, where the same appeal occurs, word for word. . .

their interchange of epithets and the alternate recurrence
of the names of the Father and the Son, to emphasize
the equality of the Persons and the Unity of the Christian
Trinity.

To the same period I would assign the Eighth Hymn, Hymn VIII.
which contains, moreover, a hint as to its date in the
allusion to his *two* children* (συνώριδα τεκέων), thus fixing
its composition before 409 A.D. The Invocation is, as
in Hymn V., to the glorious Son of the Virgin. There
is the same prayer for a life of even tenor, not unmingled
with aspirations after worldly fame. But the main interest
of the Hymn is personal. Synesius thanks God for his
brother's recovery from a dangerous illness—" Whom thou
"didst bring back," he says, "when his foot was already
"across the threshold of the lower world, and didst lull
"my cares and sorrow to rest and wipe away my tears."
Then he prays for his sister and his two children, and
last of all for his wife (one of the two allusions to her
in his writings) that she may be true to him and jealous of
her honour.

Hymns VII. IX. and X. remain—and of these the first
two naturally fall together, both referring especially to the
descent of our Lord to Hades, and the ninth markedly
blending Christian thought with Pagan imagery.

In the seventh we find the first mention of the name Hymn VII.
"Jesus." He is the Mighty God, Son of God, the Son
Creator of the World, of the Father Creator of the Ages.
His nature at once human and divine is spoken of, his
Godship and his death. His mortal birth and the star
that foretold it are alluded to, and the visit of the Magi
with the symbolical interpretation of their gifts, " Thou art
"God, receive frankincense. Gold I bear for a King.

* Synesius had three children and they were all born before he became
Bishop in 410.

Hymn IX.

"Myrrh will befit thy burial." The Hymn closes with a symbolical expression of the Omnipresence of God and the descent to Hades, which plays so prominent a part in Hymn IX. Here again, the invocation is to the blessed son of the maiden of Solyma—who drove the snake from his father's garden, who came down upon earth to dwell among men and descended into Tartarus where death holds the countless myriads of departed spirits. "Immemorial Hades shuddered at thee "and the ravening hound shrank from the threshold. But "thou, when thou hadst freed the spotless companies of souls "from their affliction, didst carry hymns of praise to the "Father on High." Then Synesius, in a passage which recalls the majestic harmonies of Milton, tells of the ascent into heaven amid the music of the spheres, as they joined in triumphal strain, while the powers of darkness trembled. "The day star smiled, and Golden Hesperus, Cythera's "star, and all nature recognized the unspeakable progress "of the Son of God." And so Christ passes to the pure region of the spheres, where is the fountain of good, and the heaven calm in silence, where time is not, or the shameless taint of matter.

Hymn X.

The tenth hymn is left. I will close this brief notice of the later Hymns by a translation of this, the last and shortest.

"Remember, O Christ, thy servant, thou Son of God "who reigns on High—thy servant the sinful author of these "strains. And grant me release from the deadly passions "implanted in my polluted heart. Grant me to see thy "radiance divine, Jesu! Saviour! Then will I sing thy "praises in thy presence, Healer of souls, Healer of bodies— "together with the Mighty Father and Holy Spirit."

(ii.) *b*. His acts as Bishop.

(ii.) *b*. Synesius' official Christianity as evidenced by his acts as Bishop.—In dealing with this second aspect of

Synesius' Christian life I shall attempt no detailed account of
his doings as Bishop of Ptolemais (that subject has been
already dealt with in the life), my present object is rather
to deduce briefly from these events the tendency they indi-
cate, avoiding as far as possible unnecessary repetition of
familiar detail.

By way of preliminary, I must repeat, at risk of tedious-
ness, that few things are more noticeable in the letters
which furnish the details for this period than the intense
respect without a touch of servility, the loyal reverence
which Synesius consistently pays to his primate Theophilus.
It is only another instance of the sterling good sense which
is so strong a point in his character that he took up at once
the attitude of a churchman, and paid to Theophilus, as his
Patriarch, the deference which he might have withheld from
him as a man.

Relations to Theophilus.

It is difficult to realise how hard and trying Synesius'
position must have been for the first few months of his
episcopate.   There he was, imperfectly versed in the scriptures he had to teach, still more ignorant of the ritual and
service, to say nothing of the laws of Church discipline.
Add to this a real reluctance to performing the routine of
business, an aversion to the practical side of life, and it will
be plain that there was no easy task before him.   The post
of bishop in those troubled times was no sinecure, and
the tendency to combine the spiritual and political functions
in the local Heads of the Church was a real moral defect
which must have been particularly galling to a contemplative
nature.

Under these circumstances it is not surprising to find
Synesius at a loss what to do on occasions.   He shows a
tendency to shrink from responsibility, to secure the advice
and cooperation of others.   This comes out especially in
the case of Andronicus, where Synesius seemed to have

Andronicus.

waited almost too long, and had all but succumbed to despair when the sense of outrage brought him to himself.

Again, in the question of the Arian heresy as held by the sect of the Eunomians. His anxiety to do the right thing and to uphold the cause of the true Church against the heretics, may be inferred from the letters of Isidore of Pelusium, which are written to enlighten Synesius on the doctrine of Nicaea.

The Eunomians.

Some difficulty has been made as to the conduct of Synesius in this matter. It has been questioned whether as a man of doubtful orthodoxy he could honestly take measures against heretics. It has been suggested that the tenets of the Eunomians would be peculiarly obnoxious to him, and that he would thus be more disposed to treat them with severity. But it is far more natural to derive his motives rather from the firm loyalty to the cause he championed, which never allowed him long to shrink from any duty. The very fact that he appends to the vigorous charge, in which he denounces these men as apostles of the devil, a strict injunction to the people not to plunder or ill-treat the interlopers—is sufficient evidence that the act was necessary for the preservation of church discipline, and that as such Synesius would not delay its execution a moment.

His relentful generosity to Andronicus, and the letter in which he pleads that ruffian's cause with Theophilus, illustrates his forgiving, and perhaps too easy-going nature. But too much stress must not be laid on this last point in Synesius' character. He could be firm when he liked, stern even, as in the condemnation of Lamponianus,* and his weakness comes out rather in the tendency to lean upon others, the inability to act alone, which sometimes landed him in strange inconsistences.

---

* Vide on page 73.

This last failing is very strikingly illustrated in the case Case of
Alexander. of Alexander.* The letter opens with an appeal to Theophilus' generous feeling. "We war not with the dead" is Synesius' apology for pleading the cause of a follower of Chrysostom. The course of action, however, which he had been pursuing, was neither fair to Alexander nor creditable to himself. In private he treated him as a friend, but publicly he ignored him, and as a Bishop denied him the rights of a churchman. Even so, people took offence, and Synesius was not strong enough to boldly override the popular prejudice in the matter. Whenever he met him on his way to Church, he looked aside and felt himself blush. The elders with whom he consulted on the matter did not help him, and Theophilus' advice, whether given or not, has not been preserved to us.

The letter however which gives us most insight into Synesius' active service as a churchman, is the long epistle to Theophilus, which contains the history of an attempt to The events at
Palaebisca. establish a Bishopric at the village of Palaebisca. Here we see Synesius at his best, especially in his decision of the dispute between the rival Bishops Paul and Dioscorus.† His judgment on the scruples raised against interfering with the former's perfunctory consecration of the fort, is a capital instance of true common sense; while his appreciation of the repentance of Paul and the generosity of Dioscorus illustrate his genial nature and his readiness to see good in others.

So far then as we can judge by the actual recorded acts Synesius.
His merits and
defects, as
Bishop. of Synesius as Bishop, he was, in spite of occasional weakness, a thoroughly capable and absolutely conscientious pastor of his Church. But while allowing to him full merit for the performance of necessary duties, we must not omit

* Vide on page 70.
† Vide on pages 72 and 73.

to notice the repeated expressions of reluctance, and almost of despair, which recur again and again in his·later letters, and show that he always found his position a sorely trying one. His last purpose, unless it became realized before his death, was to build a monastery: whither, possibly, he intended to retire in his solitary old age, and leave the uncongenial world for a life of meditation.

In any case, he never got over this reluctance, amounting almost to detestation of the practical life. His early training, his independent fortune, the philosophy he adopted, and the principles to which he clung to the last, all pointed to the life of contemplation ; and when, by some adverse, or shall we not rather say some gracious fate, stern only in true kindness, Synesius found himself ever swept into the vortex of strife and action, and weighed down in his hour of sorest need by the recurrence of domestic affliction, what can we expect but a life of conflicting aims and disappointed cravings? This thought leads up naturally to the last question for discussion.

(iii.) Internal evidence as to belief.

(iii.) Internal evidence as to Synesius' belief.—Here one is treading on more dangerous ground. It may seem hard to impugn the possibility of Synesius' Christianity, in the light of his loyalty to the Church, but there are weighty reasons for so doing, and there is only one preliminary upon which there must be no misunderstanding, that Synesius' honesty of religious purpose is nowhere called in question.

How far *could* Synesius become Christian?

We do not ask how far was Synesius' sympathy genuine, but how far it was actual and possible? Clausen is, I think, unfair in this matter to Synesius. Just as he assumes his silence on the more important points of his dissent from Christian doctrine, so in this crucial question of Synesius' life, he questions his sincerity.*

* Clausen, ap. Kraus, Tüb. Q. for 1865, pp. 545-6.

But the language of Synesius is not that of a man who feels the hollowness of acting a hypocritical part, it is rather the impatience of one who found his work unfortunately, as he foresaw it would be, uncongenial. Kraus seems to me to state the real nature of Synesius' belief in the words :—" Er mochte mit dem Wunsche seines His real "Herzens Christ sein, aber der Verstand, den man den attitude. "gebornen Heiden genannt, er war auch in ihm noch " Heide, noch Platoniker geblieben."

There are many indications of this besides the somewhat querulous appeals to Theophilus. For instance, in his speech against Andronicus,* " For all things are turning "out contrary for me, because of hazardous foolhardiness, "in that I, a man of sins, an outcast from the Church, "reared to a different scheme of life, approached the "altar of God." Still more to the point on this question is Imperfect the fact that his letters to Pagan friends show no trace nature of whatever of Christian influence. Now one cannot imagine his Faith. that a man who really appreciated the fulness and depth of the religion of Christ could escape the inspiration of that divine enthusiasm which it was Christ's mission to arouse, and which when it once entered into a man, took possession of his whole being and tinged with its ennobling influence every action of his life. To this enthusiasm Synesius was a stranger, and thus, what is otherwise inexplicable becomes clear, the fact that in his unofficial writings where he opens his heart to his friends, where the Bishop retires into the background and the real man is presented to our view, it is the Greek and the Philosopher, not the Christian, that we see.

In his famous denunciation of Andronicus, he describes the depths of despair into which the death of his child,

* Ep. 57.

added to the afflictions of his people, had plunged him. He had been all but on the verge of committing suicide. The precepts of philosophy had failed him—God gave no answer to his prayers. But he makes no allusion to the comfort of a steadfast faith in Christ with which many of his hearers must have been familiar.

It may be urged that the later hymns, the peroration of the *Catastasis*, could only have been written by a true Christian, but a careful perusal of these works in the light of Synesius' other writings shows that, though he had learned something of the phraseology, something of the doctrines of Christianity, and could express his thoughts with a beauty and an earnestness that sprang naturally from what had always been a religious mind, yet throughout his grasp of Christianity is an imperfect one, and his faith in the new creed was not such as to stand unshaken in the sore trials through which he was destined to pass.

His last letter addressed to Hypatia.

It is a striking and an instructive fact, in this connection, that what was probably Synesius' last letter, written at a time when all hope seemed gone and the bed of sickness on which he lay promised almost a welcome delivery from his distress—is addressed to Hypatia, his old instructress, the truest representative to him of the philosophy to which he still clung.

There is something unmanly to our northern notions in the absolute prostration of Synesius under trouble.* But we must remember not only the circumstances of his trials but also the characteristics of his age. It was not an age of strong faith in God. It was rather an age for men who had strong faith in themselves, the hard and the unscrupulous. The times were troubled, and the long-continued sufferings of the unhappy country of Synesius might well

* Ep. 57, 196, A-D, 197, D. Ep, 79, 227, B. Ep. 67, 217, A. Ep. 126, 261, C. Ep. 69, 217, D.

have made a bolder mind despair. Whether if he had
lived longer he might have attained a higher and a truer
notion of the Christian faith is not a question for conjecture.
All we can say is that when every allowance has been
made we still find Synesius' Christianity imperfect. And
although it would be easy to parallel the depths of his
depression from many of the Psalms, and though it might
be argued that the latter were written by men whose whole
lives had been spent in the service of the religion they pro-
fessed, and hence small wonder if a convert of so few years'
standing as Synesius found his philosophy and his religion
alike fail him, still while in the Psalms, even in the darkest
and most despairing, there ever lurks a conviction that there
is a God and a righteous God, and that his will must be
done and that the good cause will prevail, we find no
brighter side, no hint of confidence to relieve the blackness
of Synesius' despondency. The doctrine of suffering was
a mystery unsolved to him. To him the difficulties of life
were not, as they have been well called, the truest pledges
of its nobility. The old mistaken contempt for this world
and this mortal body and this daily round of necessary
duty was too deeply ingrained in his character.

The Kingdom of Heaven within us upon earth is no His false Ideal
reality for Synesius. Our life here he held to be a painful of life.
trial, to be struggled through and shuffled off as soon as
may be; and the prayer which so constantly recurs in the
Hymns is not for the cheerful performance of duty here
below as the source of true happiness, not for the love that
may fill us with sympathy for our fellow-creatures, and the
faith which maketh not afraid, but an entreaty for a life free
from mental cares and bodily ills—a sort of blissful calm
that will leave the mind free to soar where it will in loftiest
contemplation, that so by abstraction from the sphere of
the material, and avoidance of the taint of its contact, it

may complete its weary term of bondage in this earthly prison house, and merge itself in union with the Eternal source from which it sprang.

Reasons for his failure. A selfish retirement, an Epicurean freedom from pain, a mystic union as the final goal of a useless but inevitable period of existence—this was no ideal to sustain a man in the hour of trouble, or to fit him for doing his duty in practical life. But once more, in conclusion, we must confess that though Synesius falls short of the Christian Ideal, and only imperfectly appreciated the value of the Christian faith, yet he was still immeasurably superior to the philosophy he upheld ; and, although reluctantly, still, **How far to be called a failure.** with a conscientiousness that is the more to his credit, he did give up the life of ease and retirement to which his every instinct inclined him, and the worst that can be said of him is only this, that the old Adam in his nature was imperfectly eradicated, that he repined at times in the fulfilment of his duty and broke down under the stress of misfortune because his old Faith was inadequate to sustain him and his new Faith too imperfect to supply the need.

CONCLUSION.

CONCLUSION.

In concluding this sketch of Synesius' life and writings, three questions call for a brief answer—brief, because under different forms they have been discussed to the best of my ability in these pages. What are we to say of Synesius as a writer, as a thinker, and as a Christian?

As a writer he is undoubtedly at his best in the letters, which are singularly attractive, and deserve to be more widely known. They reveal to us a personality, if not of a great, at all events of a lovable man, and from a historical point of view throw a valuable light on the customs of the Church and people in that age. Synesius was of too pliable and unimpassioned a nature to produce any striking literary work, but there are times when he rises above his usually calm mood, and, stirred by the apathy of the Court or the outrages of Andronicus, gives utterance to burning words of true eloquence.

Next to the letters, in interest and originality, I would place the Hymns. Apart from the earnest spirit which breathes through every line, there are occasional flashes of real poetry, and they are moreover especially important in tracing the growth of Synesius' inner thought, to which they form a kind of running commentary. As a thinker, Synesius was by no means original, nor indeed was the philosophy which served him for a creed. It would be absurd to expect from a Neo-Platonist of the fourth century any new development of thought, for the philosophy of the schools was already stereotyped when Synesius sat at the feet of Hypatia.

Lastly, Synesius as a Christian. Here it must be confessed boldly that Synesius owed very little, as far as we

J

can judge, to Christianity. All the best traits in his character shine out quite as clearly in the years preceding his conversion. And though, indirectly, of course he owed much to the religion which for nigh four centuries had been insensibly leavening the thoughts and actions of mankind ; still from a comparison of his life before and after he became bishop, the force of the statement will be made clear that the finest elements of his nature were the outcome of his birth and training, and not of the religion which he so imperfectly embraced in the closing years of a short life.

It has been said that the world knows nothing of its greatest men—possibly it knows too much in these days of biography—but in the past it is certainly the case that the men who have formed their age and opened new eras for mankind have often been unrecognized till their work was done and the result of it apparent. To this class Synesius does not belong, but rather to that larger body of men who present to us in their mental development the shifting tendencies, the half-expressed longings of their age. And following out this idea, we see that Synesius' faith is like the faith of his age, transitional, and so, imperfect. There could hardly be a more striking instance of a man moulded by the influences of his time and moving in harmony with its tendency. Paganism was fast paling before the rising power of Christianity, but it was not yet extinguished in Synesius' lifetime. Synesius becomes a Christian, but the Paganism in which he was brought up had struck too deep root in his nature to be supplanted. Neo-Platonism practically ended with Hypatia, and Synesius' life closed probably in the year before her death. And just as the imperfection of Synesius' acceptance of Christianity was a necessity of the time, so his literary vanity and the dilletante tendency of his thought were the faults not of his character so much as of his age. It is a strange thought, yet a true one, that had Synesius' life not been cast in a sphere where he was forced into action, he might have gone on dabbling in philosophy and writing such works as the *Calvitii Encomium* to the end of his days.

But enough has been said of the shortcomings of Synesius as a writer, as a thinker, and as an exponent of the Christian faith. After all, the great thing about the man is his life, and the genial good-nature which makes his letters such delightful reading, and earned for them a popularity which they still deserve. One may safely say of Synesius that he made friends wherever he went, and that he never lost one through any fault of his own. It is true that this was largely owing to the gentle element in his nature, which made it hard for him to stand alone, and which at times proved a source of weakness under trial. Thus the frequent letters of reproach to his friends for not writing to him, his confession to an almost womanish despair when all that he loved best had left him,* all point to a nature that leaned much upon others and was lacking in sturdy independence. But while this gentleness of disposition made Synesius too susceptible, it was also the source of that moderation and readiness to forgive which secured the happiness of his household, and saved even an Andronicus from the extremities of the law. It was the same spirit of moderation that prevented him from becoming a gloomy ascetic and made him a hearty country gentleman, with a genuine love of sport and a keen enjoyment of out-door life which counteracted the solitary tendencies of his philosophy. But above all, the active part he took in the defence of his country, his restless energy in coping with the barbarians, which kept him scouring the

* Epp. 56 and 79.

country for days in the saddle or taking his turn on watch through the weary hours of night on the walls of Cyrene or Ptolemais, all proved that he was possessed of true courage and endurance.

Lastly, when we remember that the ideal of his life was a peaceful unbroken calm of philosophic leisure, varied by the simple amusements of a rural life, when we read his reiterated prayer for a life free from pain or trouble, of pure contemplation unbroken by the worries of business and action ; then we must surely confess that the self-sacrifice which never allowed him to rest while his country or his flock was in danger, was indeed worthy of the Christian faith. And if under the stress of disaster, the horrors of war, the hopeless ruin of his country, and, in the midst of these, the loss by death of all that he held most dear ; if in such unheard-of trials Synesius appears to succumb to despair and to find no comfort in philosophic reflection or religious faith, let the voice of criticism be silent, and let the apparent weakness of his dying hours find an ample apology in the true nobility of a devoted life.

FINIS.

Printed by Hall and English, High Street, Birmingham.